Good
l

Enterprise and Venture Ca

GW01005426

Enterprise and Venture Capital

a business builders' and investors' handbook

Christopher C. Golis, MA MSc FSIA

ALLEN & UNWIN

First published in 1989
Second edition published in 1993

Allen & Unwin Pty Ltd
9 Atchison Street, St Leonards, NSW 2065 Australia

National Library of Australia
Cataloguing-in-Publication entry:

Golis, Christopher C.
  Enterprise and venture capital:
  a business builders' and investors' handbook.

  2nd ed.
  Bibliography
  Includes index.

  ISBN 1 86373 354 X.

  1. Entrepreneurship–Australia. 2. Venture capital–
  Australia 3. Business enterprises–Australia. I. Title.

338.040994

Set in 10/12 pt Garamond by DOCUPRO, Sydney
Printed in Singapore by Chong Moh Offset Printing Pte Ltd

10 9 8 7 6 5 4 3 2

Contents

Tables

Figures

Glossary

(Readers will find Edna Carew's *The Language of Money*, published by Allen & Unwin, a useful reference guide.)

Add-ons Marketing term used to describe the extra charges and fees added to the basic price of a product.

Affirmative covenants Terms contained in a shareholders' agreement where the company or management agree to carry out certain actions. Examples would be to prepare annual budgets and supply monthly accounts.

Aftermarket support Term used to describe the activities of a broker or underwriter after a listing to ensure the share price remains steady or rises. This can vary from acting as a principal buying shares to demanding immediate payment of the underwriting fees.

Agency capture What happens when politicians full of good intent instead of using the threat of competition create a bureaucratic agency to protect consumers. The major suppliers then capture the agency and change it into a lobbying agent among the politicians.

Aquaculture Growing crops in water rather than on land. Agriculture has been in existence for about 10,000 years and aquaculture 100 years, which is a reasonable insight into the risks involved.

Asset redeployment Term used by new owners of a company to explain how they intend to improve the return on assets. For example actions might include selling businesses which are not an intrinsic part of the business, rationalising product lines and so forth.

Asset turn The ratio obtained when the annual sales are divided by the assets of the company. The ratio can vary from one for a miner to say eight for a retailer.

Blue chips In Australia the top one hundred companies ranked by market capitalisation which would be able to borrow unsecured from banks and whose shares would be an automatic choice in most institutional portfolios.

Breakeven analysis Financial tool which is used to establish if the gross profit of a business will exceed the fixed costs.

Buy-in price Price at which an investor purchases new shares for transactions where the cash remains within the company.

Buy-out price Price at which an investor purchases old shares for transactions where the cash goes with the seller.

Call option A contract whereby the holder of the option has the right to buy from the grantor shares at a specific price (strike price) at some time in the future.

Capital employed Capital employed is the sum of equity and long term debt used by a company to purchase long term assets and for working capital.

Capital turn The ratio obtained by dividing the annual sales of a company by the capital employed.

Cold call presentation Selling term used to describe the first meeting between a buyer and seller where the initial contact has been at most a telephone call arranging a meeting.

Contributing shares Shares on which only part of the capital amount and any premium has been paid. Often useful in tranching structures.

Contribution rate Accounting term expressed as a percentage calculated by subtracting the variable costs from sales. The contribution rate then describes what percentage of each sales dollar is available to cover fixed costs.

Convertible notes Hybrid fixed interest security whereby the holder has the option of converting the debt to equity at some pre-arranged date and conversion price.

Convertible preference shares Preference shares which may be converted to ordinary shares at the option of the holder.

Cost of goods sold Accounting term defined by the equation opening stock plus purchases plus expenses related to purchases less closing stock.

Deal flow Venture capital term used to describe the number of proposals being received by a venture capital fund on some calendar basis such as three deals a week.

Dilution of equity Stock market term used to describe the situation whereby the issue of new shares results in the original shareholders owning a smaller share of the company.

Dividend yield Stockmarket term which expresses as percentage return the annual dividend per share divided by the latest market price.

Entitlement issue See non-renounceable rights issue.

Earnouts Venture capital term used to describe the technique whereby the management or owners increase their ownership or sell-out price according to the profits they produce over some period.

Economies of scale Economic term used to describe the cost benefits that accrue from increasing size such as volume discounts on purchases or spreading fixed costs over an increasingly larger production base.

Equity The proportion of a company that shareholders own. Sometimes described as shareholders' funds.

Equity kicker Shares or call options offered to either lenders, underwriters, promoters or management as additional consideration for services rendered.

Equity sweetener Effectively the same as equity kicker but generally used when referring to free options granted to subscribers to a new issue of shares.

Escrow provisions Legal term used to describe undertaking given by present shareholders not to sell shares unless certain conditions are met.

Exit mechanism Venture capital term used to describe the method by which a venture capitalist will eventually sell out of an investment.

Financing gap Venture capital term used in leveraged buyouts to describe difference between the purchase price of a company and the debt raised on the assets and cash flow of the company.

Fire sale Finance term used to describe the situation when a company is forced to sell off assets cheaply because of lack of cash.

Fixed costs Those costs such as rent that do not vary according to changes in sales levels.

Floor Stock market term used to describe the situation where a buyer has a permanent order in to buy shares at a certain price.

Franked dividend Dividend paid out of after tax profits on which tax at the full corporate rate (presently 39 per cent) has been paid. Recipients of franked dividends are not subject to further taxation on the dividend.

Gearing The ratio of debt to equity as stated in a company's balance sheet.

Golden share A share whose vote must be included in any motion passed by the shareholders.

Gross profit Sales less cost of goods sold.

Hurt money Cash invested or exposure made by an entrepreneur to the business. The greater the proportion hurt money represents of the entrepreneur's personal wealth the more convincing the argument to the investor.

Identifiable intangibles Intangible assets for which it is possible to set a valuation such as future income tax benefit.

Illiquid Term used to describe an investment for which there are few buyers.

Implementation plan Plan defining the steps and activities required to achieve goals.

Intangible assets Assets owned or generated by a company that are not easily sold except with the company as a whole and usually are not easily measurable.

Intellectual property Legal term used to describe the patents, licences, copyrights, trademarks and designs owned by a company.

Interest cover Pre-interest cash flow divided by interest payments.

Learning curve An imaginary curve which describes the reduction in cost that occurs as a factory makes more and more of a particular product. Also used to describe the increase in skill of an employee over time.

Letter of intent Document which is not legally binding but given by one party to another to show good faith and which describes the main agreed points of a transaction.

Leveraged buy-out Purchase of a company where the purchaser uses a larger than normal amount of debt to finance the transaction.

Living dead Term used by venture capitalists to describe investments which while not decreasing in value are showing no growth.

Management buy-out Usually a leveraged buy-out organised by the existing management of the company.

Market capitalisation Value of a company calculated by multiplying the number of shares on issue by the last sale price.

Mexican standoff Term in a shareholders' agreement which states that a shareholder who offers to buy shares from another is obliged to sell to the other party at the same price. The clause is used to ensure any offer is fair and reasonable.

Mezzanine financing Financing obtained using instruments that fall between the bottom floor of equity and the top floor of secured debt.

Monopolistic competition Industry structure where there are many small suppliers each of which has a monopoly position in the area it serves.

Negative covenants Terms in a shareholders' agreement that state actions the management of a company may not carry out without the permission of the investors or their representatives. Examples include changes in executives' salary levels and sales of major fixed assets.

Negative pledge Lending agreement where the borrower covenants are not to exceed certain limits such as gearing levels.

Net profit Sales, less all expenses which may or may not include corporate tax.

Net tangible assets The difference between tangible assets (e.g. stock, debtors, land etc.) and liabilities in the balance sheet.

Net worth The difference between the assets and liabilities of a company on its balance sheet. Net worth is equal to the shareholder funds.

Non-price competition Competition among suppliers using such items as warranty periods, credit terms, and after sales service.

Non-renounceable rights issue Rights issue where the shareholders may either take up rights or let them lapse. The shareholders are not allowed to sell the rights to another party. Also known as an entitlement issue.

Oligopolistic structure Industry structure where a few suppliers dominate the market.

Owner's equity The residual of assets less external liabilities.

Partly paid shares See 'Contributing shares'.

P/E ratio Price/earnings ratio. The ratio of share price to earning per share.

Petty patent Special patent that allows the inventor to only protect one aspect of an invention for only a short period of time (five years) but is less expensive and obtained within six months.

Portfolio diversification Investment strategy where the portfolio manager spreads investments across many industries and thus tries to diminish the risk of a single industry depression reducing the portfolio return.

Positioning strategy Marketing term used to define a strategy where a company tries to distinguish itself from its competitors by focusing on some market segment.

Post-funding valuation Valuation of company after an equity injection that is obtained by multiplying the total shares on issue by the share purchase price.

Preference shares Shares that rank ahead of ordinary shares for dividends or payment upon winding up of the company.

Pre-funding valuation The valuation of the company prior to funding calculated by subtracting the cash that remains within the company from the post-funding valuation.

Price taker Marketing term used to describe a supplier of goods whose price is set independently by the market.

Price-to-book value ratio The ratio of the share price to the net worth per share.

Price-to-revenue ratio The ratio of the share price to the company revenues per share.

Pro forma accounts Balance sheets and profit and loss statements for future years prepared in the same format as the current accounts.

Product differentiation Marketing term used to describe strategy of defining new or current product features or benefits that distinguish it from the competition.

Put option A contract whereby the holder of the option has the right to sell to the grantor shares at a specific price (strike price) at some time in the future.

Ride Venture capital term used to describe the potential percentage of profits or equity ownership available if a deal works out as planned.

Redeemable preference shares Preference shares which at a stated maturity date will be redeemed by the issuing company.

Revalued asset Asset assigned some value other than the book value (cost price less any depreciation). Revaluations may be either downwards (investments devalued to market price) or upwards (e.g. real estate or directors revaluation of licence agreements).

Rights issue An issue of new shares on a proportional basis to existing shareholders usually at a discount to market price to raise additional shareholders' funds. The shareholder may allow the offer to lapse or if the issue is renounceable sell or transfer the rights to another party.

Road show presentation Series of presentations made to institutional and large private investors to sell a new issue.

Running yield The return on an investment expressed as cash earned over cash invested. No account is taken of potential capital gain on redemption.

Second line stock Shares of listed companies that do not rank as blue chip or first line companies.

Secured debt Loan, where the lender, in the event of a failure to meet either an interest or principal payment, gains title to an asset.

Secured lending Making loans only to parties who can provide an asset as security in the event of non-payment of interest or principal.

Seller's note Sometimes known as vendor finance where the seller of the asset accepts some part of the payment on deferred terms.

Sensitivity analysis Financial analysis where variables such as selling price are adjusted upwards and downwards by some factor (say 20 per cent) to establish the effect on profits.

Shelf company A company which has been created but never traded.

Shortfall The difference in a fund raising between the expected amount and amount actually raised which in turn must be provided by the underwriters.

Stag profits Profits made by someone who subscribes to a new issue and sells on the first day of trading.

Strike price The price of the underlying share at which a call or put option is exercisable.

Subordinated debt A loan which ranks behind other debts if a company is wound up. Subordinated loans, if provided by a venture capitalist, would either command a higher interest rate or have call options attached.

Suppliers' credit Often overlooked form of financing provided by creditors when they offer extended payment terms.

Takeout mechanism See 'Exit mechanism'.

Taking a bath Slang term used by an investor who has seen a significant reduction in value of an investment or an underwriter faced with a significant shortfall.

Technology parks Industrial estates located next to universities or other research establishments and designed to attract advanced technology companies.

Term sheet A short two or three page document that outlines the investment agreement between an entrepreneur and investors.

Tranching Investment made in stages; each stage being dependent on achievement of targets.

Trial close Selling term used to describe when a salesperson asks for the order not expecting success but hoping to unearth further objections from the prospect.

Turnaround Company converted from making losses to profits. A turnaround situation is a company which is still making losses but which an investor believes has sufficient turnover to make potential profits.

Undercapitalisation Situation for a company where insufficient equity has been supplied by the shareholders or retained in the company to support the activities of the business.

Unsecured lending Lending where the borrower has not provided any assets in the event of non-payment of interest or principal.

Uprates Marketing term used to describe upward revisions in pricing schedules.

Vapourware Computer industry term used to describe non-existent products compared to actual hardware and software.

Variable cost Costs such as materials and manufacturing labour that vary with the level of sales.

Warranties Terms in shareholders' agreement whereby the promoter or vendor guarantee the past and present operating condition of a company. Examples include operating in a legal fashion; no bad debts or stock etc. Breach of warranty gives the investor the right to claim damages but does not destroy the contract.

Working Capital Capital employed by the company to fund the excess of current assets (stock, debtors etc.) over current liabilities (creditors, leave provisions, bank overdraft etc.)

Acronyms

ABS	Australian Bureau of Statistics
AIDC	Australian Industry Development Corporation
ARD	American Research and Development
ASX	Australian Stock Exchange
ATG	Australian Technology Group
BLEC	BLE Capital (formerly Business Loans and Equity Capital Ltd)
CAC	Corporate Affairs Commission
CDB	Commonwealth Development Bank
COGS	Cost of Goods Sold
CSR	CSR Limited
DEC	Digital Equipment Corporation
EBIT	Earnings Before Interest and Taxation
EMDG	Export Market Development Grants Scheme
ESOPs	Employee Stock Ownership Plans
ESOT	Employee Share Ownership Trust
FAI	FAI Insurances
FIRST	Funding for Innovation Research and State Technology
GIRD	Grants for Industrial Research and Development
IAC	Industries Assistance Commission
IPO	Initial Public Offering
ITES	International Trade Enhancement Scheme
LBO	Leveraged Buy-out
MIC	Management and Investment Companies
NEIS	New Enterprise Incentive Scheme
NIES	National Industry Extension Service
NPDP	National Procurement Development Program
NSWIC	New South Wales Investment Corporation
PDF	Pooled Development Fund
PMA	Positive Mental Attitude

R&D	Research and Development
ROCE	Return on Capital Employed
ROE	Return on Equity
SBIC	Small Business Investment Corporation
USM	Unlisted Securities Market
USP	Unique Selling Proposition
VCF	Venture Capital Fund
VEDC	Victorian Economic Development Corporation

Acknowledgements

I first became interested in the Australian venture capital arena in the most practical way in May 1984 when successfully selling investors on the idea by way of the BT Innovation Limited prospectus. My appetite whetted, I have since worked full-time in the fledgling industry. I became a venture capital groupie and devoured a host of reading matter about the industry. Three books are of particular importance: Brandt's *Entrepreneuring: The Ten Commandments*, Lipper's *Investing in Private Companies*, and Silver's *Venture Capital, The Complete Guide for Investors*. All three are recommended reading for anyone wishing to increase their knowledge about this subject.

On the practical level I would like to thank the authors of the 800 business plans I have read so far and the dozen entrepreneurs who were selected for investment. All of us have learned a lot. For this second edition my new computer, MicroSoft Windows and MicroSoft Word for Windows were invaluable. John Legge of the Swinburne Institute of Technology played an important role in getting this book published and his revisions to chapter 12 were gratefully accepted. I would also like to thank Clare McAdam and Mark Tredinnick.

Once again I thank my daughters, Louisa and Laura, and my wife, Vivienne, for their encouragement and patience.

Finally, the proviso of the first edition still stands. I have taken all care to ensure the information contained in this book is true at the time of publication. However I cannot represent the information as accurate or complete because of the changes that are continually occurring in the business, government, financial, legislative, and taxation environments. The changes in the four years since the first edition are significant. Readers should not use or rely on this book as a substitute for detailed advice or as a basis for formulating business decisions.

Introduction
Playing the game

Venture capital in the sense of financing new ventures has existed throughout history. One of the most famous examples was the financing by Queen Isabella of Spain of Christopher Columbus's expedition to the New World in 1492. Before receiving funding from the Queen, Columbus wandered around offices of the venture capitalists of the time, namely the courts of Europe, seeking finance for what must have appeared a ridiculous venture. The business plan, to sail three ships due west across the Atlantic, was based on the self-evidently absurd hypothesis that the world was round. The results were beyond Isabella's wildest expectations. The mineral wealth extracted from the New World laid the foundations for the Spanish domination of Europe for the next 100 years.

The ad hoc support of ventures was converted to systematic work, that is, an industry, by the Americans after World War II. General Doriot, a French émigré and influential professor at the Harvard Business School during the 1930s, rose to the rank of Brigadier General during World War II. After the war, he founded the first venture capital company, American Research and Development (ARD). In 1956 General Doriot made one of the more satisfactory venture capital investments—a minority investment of $70 000 in a fledgling company started by a young engineer, Kenneth Olsen. Over the next fourteen years, Doriot guided Olsen and his company until by 1971 the $70 000 investment was valued at $350 million. Olsen's idea was to connect two inventions, the television and the batch computer, and produce an 'interactive' computer. The company was Digital Equipment Corporation. The annualised compound return on the investment was 84 per cent.

This book deals with true entrepreneurs, the builders of businesses, and venture capital from an Australian perspective. While Australia has had a long tradition of business-building entrepreneurs, the formal venture capital industry started officially in May 1984 with the beginning of the government-sponsored Management and Investment Company Program. Since then there has been a burst of venture capital activity.

In this book we will examine in detail entrepreneurs and venture capital intermediaries. While the number of successful entrepreneurs and professional venture capitalists in Australia is small, the concepts discussed in this book have far wider applications. Among the people who should find this book of use are students of business and commerce, private investors, and those people who wish to start or run their own business.

This book is aimed at people working in and building growth companies. It is not aimed at consultants or people running shops or restaurants. Nevertheless, the principles enunciated in this book will be helpful in analysing the potential success of a small business.

Reading this book will not automatically make you rich. The primary requirements for a successful business remain a receptive market, a significant competitive advantage, sufficient capital, good people, tenacity and luck. Nevertheless, if reading this book does not make you rich it could well stop you becoming poor. Although I still regard myself as a novice in venture capital I am still amazed by the time, effort and money invested in products or services that have little or limited chance of success. I am further distressed at how poor organisation and financial structure has ruined potentially excellent ideas.

The book is divided into five parts. The first part deals with entrepreneurs and tries to teach them how to analyse markets, products and the financials of a company. It ends with a chapter on the easiest way of getting to run your own business, which is to take over an existing company. Unfortunately the word 'entrepreneur' has acquired negative connotations. In Australia, instead of meaning a business-builder as it does in other parts of the English-speaking world, it now has derogatory associations and has become synonymous with hustling wheeler-dealers. The fault for this shift in meaning is due in part to the business media but also the Australian Stock Exchange, which created an index called Entrepreneurial Stocks. This was composed of companies which, provided with easy money from the banks, paid excessive amounts for listed companies and then ran them poorly.

The second part of the book looks at the spectrum of

venture capital available. Again, unfortunately, in Australia the term 'venture capital' has become synonymous with high technology business start-ups. Overseas the term covers not only start-up and seed capital, but also development capital to fund growth, and acquisition capital for buy-outs. Simply put, *venture capital may be regarded as an equity investment where investors expect significant capital gains in return for accepting the risk that they may lose all their equity*. Typically the investment is either in a privately held company or a publicly listed company that has just started and does not have a track record of producing dividends for investors. The other major form of venture capital investment is in the leveraged buy-out of stable, mature businesses. Here the buy-out is financed with a larger than usual proportion of debt, placing the equity component in a correspondingly riskier position. The final chapter of the second part examines leveraged and management buy-out financing.

Part III is about the nexus between the entrepreneur and the investor. It teaches the entrepreneur what form of investment vehicle to choose, how to prepare a business plan attractive to investors, what entrepreneurs should look for in a business, and how to negotiate with prospective investors.

Part IV reverses roles and examines the issues from the viewpoint of the investor. The investor is taught what makes a successful investment, how to investigate a proposal, how to do valuations and structure shareholdings,what investor involvement should occur after investing, and finally how to exit from an investment.

The final part of the book is aimed at those investors who are in the fortunate position of having more than one investment and describes the requirements and idiosyncrasies of managing a venture capital fund.

We live in the most rapidly changing period of human history. When I was first learning the craft of selling, a key lesson was that change in an organisation usually meant opportunity for the sales people. As entrepreneurs make products that people buy, change favours the entrepreneur even more than the sales people.

Numerous studies have shown how wealth is concentrated in few hands. Typically 20 per cent of the population of a country controls 80 per cent of the wealth. What is not often realised is the turnover within the 20 per cent. By definition the entrepreneurs of tomorrow are the young unknown people of today. Those who learn today how to play the game are the ones who will dislodge the current occupants of the top 20 per cent and have fun in the process.

PART I

STARTING A BUSINESS

1 The entrepreneur: have you got what it takes?

When trying to establish whether you are an entrepreneur, you need to distinguish between entrepreneurs and entrepreneurial tendencies. A useful analogy is to compare an artist with a person who has artistic tendencies. There are many people with artistic tendencies. These individuals visit museums and galleries, attend auctions and collect, or perhaps go to art and craft classes. On the other hand, few people have the necessary combination of creativity, talent and persistence to call themselves artists. In a similar fashion one can distinguish between natural entrepreneurs and people with entrepreneurial tendencies.

However, it is easier to become an entrepreneur than an artist. Many more people can satisfy the requirements of the entrepreneur than those of the artist. It is easier to be a successful businessperson than a successful opera singer.

Let us begin by considering some of the characteristics of entrepreneurs. One feature is a high energy level. Entrepreneurs as a group get up early in the morning. Entrepreneurs hate to stay in bed. They tend to be enthusiastic people who realise that the only thing more contagious than enthusiasm is the lack of it.

The next quality is an interest in money. Natural entrepreneurs tend to have had jobs in childhood and understand naturally the value of money and how to use it as a resource.

The third characteristic is a creative attitude towards obstacles. When faced with obstacles, typical entrepreneurs find new ways of overcoming them. Most people are conservative. They do not like changes and prefer life to become a habit. Consequently, most people respond to proposals for change with resistance and doubt. The role of entrepreneurs is to create new businesses. They conflict with this widespread conservatism. Most people are constantly putting obstacles in the paths of entrepreneurs trying to achieve their goals. The ability to overcome these obstacles with creative solutions and do it again and again and still maintain enthusiasm is a sign of an entrepreneur.

A concept which may be familiar to some readers is Positive Mental Attitude (PMA for short). PMA has long been put forward as a cure for poor sales performance, if not the world's ills. Optimistic tenacity can be a most useful weapon. I remember a top salesmen telling me he liked getting the first refusal from a prospect. His reason was that, because it usually takes five trial closes to make a sale, when he received his first refusal he knew he had only four more closes to go. What distinguishes the entrepreneur from the average salesperson is that while the salesperson returns repeatedly with the same closing technique and fails, the entrepreneur comes up with a new design to overcome the obstacle and often succeeds.

Phillip Kahn, founder of Borland International, one of the top five computer software companies in the world, has described how in 1983, when his company developed its first software product, there were no funds available for advertising. He wanted to put a full page in the computer magazine *Byte* but the cost was $20 000. Before the advertising salesperson arrived, he hired two extra temporary staff members and arranged for his friends to ring the office constantly during the meeting. He also had on his desk a media plan for all the computer magazines, with *Byte* crossed out. The salesperson 'inadvertently' noticed the omission and asked why. He was told the media plan was done and that *Byte's* readers were not the right audience. After a few moments' persuasion Kahn reluctantly agreed to place a one-page advertisement on deferred payment terms. The advertisement generated $150 000 worth of business and the rest is history.

Entrepreneurs are famous for their risk-taking ability. It is my experience that successful entrepreneurs are not risk-takers compared with gamblers or speculators. Entrepreneurs usually operate on stretched resources, carrying out a realistic evaluation of the risks. They try to establish a position where the risk is limited and the reward is substantial. In other words they tend to look at risk–reward ratios while gamblers think only of the rewards.

The four qualities of enthusiasm, creative tendency, calculated risk-taking and energy are essential to entrepreneurs. You can establish whether you have these qualities in sufficient degree by taking on positions where they are required. At the same time you will gain further skills and experience. The most common reason for rejection of a business plan is inadequate management. This alone covers a multitude of reasons for rejection. However, the proven ability to sell is most important. At least three to four years employment in sales and sales management, particularly in the area of corporate goods or corporate services, would be useful in this context. Corporate selling is useful because the selling cycle typically takes several months and usually requires a multi-level sale. The buying organisation contains a number of decision-makers and recommenders and salespeople's success depends on their style of communicating with these various individuals working at different levels in the organisation. Running a business requires the same communication skills plus the ability to negotiate with and analyse people. Not only are these skills necessary when dealing with customers, but similar skills are required when recruiting and motivating employees. The financiers, be they banks, finance companies or venture capitalists, are as important as the customers and employees. The biographies of many successful entrepreneurs demonstrate either a natural selling ability or several years learning the skills of selling.

A good entrepreneur is typically a good communicator and is interested in the English language. Most are excellent communicators in the written form and write business letters in strong, simple English. One reason venture capitalists prefer a business plan to be produced by the entrepreneur rather than the financial adviser is that the plan then provides a good indication of the communication skills of the entrepreneur.

The next skill one likes to see in the entrepreneur is an understanding of numbers. A businessman needs to understand the principles of accounting. Gauss, one of the greatest mathematicians who ever lived, called double-entry bookkeeping the greatest mathematical achievement of mankind. I am constantly amazed to meet the number of potential entrepreneurs who do not understand the basic principles of balance sheets, profit and loss accounts, cash flows, etc. Far too many entrepreneurs leave the figures to their accountants. Successful entrepreneurs understand how to read and analyse reports. Articles about entrepreneurs often describe how they started in business by working at selling jobs during the day and studying accounting at night. Night courses in accounting are available at many institutions.

In addition, the Securities Institute of Australia has produced an excellent home study course on understanding company reports. Once you understand how to read company reports the next stage is to learn how to analyse them. In later chapters we will discuss some of the most useful techniques of financial analysis, but just reading these chapters is inadequate. The way to learn financial analysis is to actually do it and have money riding on the result.

One way to achieve this understanding is to invest small amounts of money in two or three public companies and develop the habit of both recording and analysing their progress. Over time you will develop a feel for the ratios and structures that represent a successful company.

Another skill the entrepreneur needs is an understanding of financial structuring, a topic dealt with more fully in later chapters. Entrepreneurs should be familiar with the difference between equity and debt, the roles and responsibilities of directors and the law governing companies. Another aspect of the legal process that the entrepreneurs must understand is the law of contract. This is most easily learned when working as a salesperson, but again there are simple books and courses run by such bodies as the Institute of Directors.

Another way of gaining entrepreneurial experience is to attend the Enterprise Workshop, a nine-month program that starts every February. The Enterprise Workshop operates independently in each state and is funded by a combination of government grants, corporate sponsorship and participants' fees. Participants first learn how to prepare a business plan. They then form groups and prepare a business plan for an actual invention. The plans are judged in a state competition and the state winners entered into a national competition. Several successful companies were conceived at Enterprise Workshops.

The best preparation an entrepreneur can have is to work as a general manager in charge of a profit-centre for a large company. Several years learning the disciplines of profit centre management are invaluable. As one entrepreneur put it, perhaps the best training experience for budding entrepreneurs would be to run a fish and chip shop.

2 The market: how to analyse it

In 1962 *The Structure of Scientific Revolutions* by Thomas S. Kuhn was published. This book effectively demolished the commonly held view of science as an objective progression towards the truth. Instead Kuhn established a different philosophy. He said each science had several theories that were widely accepted by nearly all the scientists involved. They conducted continuous experiments 'confirming' these generally held theories. This type of work he called 'normal' science. Gradually more and more experiments would generate complications that would destroy a theory's initial simple elegance. Then, inevitably, an individual would put forward a radical new theory, which would explain all the earlier idiosyncrasies but would meet violent opposition from the established scientific community. Kuhn called this the paradigm shift. Afterwards, when the new paradigm was accepted, the scientists would rewrite the history of their discipline to reinforce the idea of steady progression.

Business too has its paradigm shifts. Two of the more famous would be the introduction of double-entry bookkeeping in the sixteenth century and joint stock companies in the seventeenth. In the twentieth century there have been several paradigm shifts, including the introduction of the marketing concept. The previous paradigm was based on production. Provided the product worked and the price was reasonable, businesspeople assumed the product would automatically sell. Henry Ford best summed up the production philosophy in a statement about the Model T automobile: The customers could have any colour, he said, as long as it was black.

The marketing concept

The marketing concept takes the opposite view. Successful

businesspeople continually examine and investigate their markets and develop products to satisfy customers' needs. The president of Revlon epitomised the marketing philosophy when he said, 'In the factory Revlon makes lipstick, but in the marketplace it sells hope.'

In the next two chapters we will explain some simple techniques for analysing markets and products. This is not meant to be comprehensive but it should provide the aspiring entrepreneur with the means of testing whether a product has a role in the marketplace.

The economic institutions of the world have expended much time and effort on analysing markets. A classic rule of business success is to copy those practices and policies that contribute to your competitor's success. Let us now examine the methods by which economists analyse a market.

Demand and supply analysis is basic to the procedure. Indeed, an old dictum of economists tells them to remember they have two eyes—one for demand and the other for supply. Let us first look at demand analysis, by which economists try to establish what is the demand type for the product, the market size, the growth rates, and the buyer trends.

Demand analysis

Step 1 Establish the demand type

Typically the economist divides demand into three types: consumer, distributor and producer. The most familiar is consumer demand. The demographics of consumers are well known and well documented. Not only are population and dwelling statistics available but so are the results of expenditure surveys, etc. It is thus easy to evaluate consumer demand for many products.

To take a simple example, a new shopping mall has shop premises available and you and a friend wish to set up a women's clothing boutique. The area is middle-class. On a map you draw up the catchment area for your shop. First you draw a series of midpoints between the mall and the surrounding competitive malls and then a rough circle joining up the midpoints. The next step is to establish the number of households in the area. This is done by ringing up the local council that makes up the largest segment of your catchment area and finding out how many domestic rate notices it sends. You multiply this number by the inverse ratio of the local council area to the catchment area to establish the total number of households in the catchment area. Your calculations indicate there are 19 000 households. The latest Household Expenditure Survey states that the average weekly expenditure per household on women's clothing was $6.90. A few seconds on a calculator tells you the total expenditure in your catchment area is $6.8 million. Adjusting for inflation gives a total market of $8.75 million. There are 36 shops in your catchment area. Add your shop and assume everything else is equal, and you have potential annual sales of $237 000. Of course all things are not equal; establishing the degree of inequality is the subject of the next chapter.

The next type of demand is distributor demand. The bath gel discussed below is a product which is primarily driven by distributor demand. Entrepreneurs must compete with thousands of other products for shelf space and convince shopkeepers their product will provide a higher return.

The final type of demand is producer or industrial demand. This refers to the demand of companies or governments for products or services that help them produce products for the marketplace. Raw materials, business computers and merchant banking are examples of products whose sales are determined by producer demand.

Step 2 Establish the size of the market

The next question is how big is the market for the business entity? A common reason for business failure is overestimation of the size of the market and inclusion in the market estimate of prospects who would never buy anything from the business entity.

To establish the size of the market you need a clear picture in your mind of the person who is going to buy your product. Let us assume you have the opportunity to obtain Australian distribution rights for a new form of imported bath gel that retails for $15 a bottle, each bottle lasting about three months. Despite large expenditures on advertising and marketing it is difficult to envisage a household having more than one bottle of gel at a time. Thus you could define the potential market as all the households in Australia (say 5 million). One estimate for potential annual sales would be $120 million.

The next question to ask yourself is which households would buy your product? Since bath gel is a luxury or fad item bought by the upper-income households, the potential market is now reduced to, say, 10–20 per cent of households in Australia, with potential sales of $12 million – $25 million.

But you will not be selling direct to the households. You will sell to retail pharmacies of which there are 5400. They will want a 50 per cent mark-up on this product and will provide an initial order of only a dozen bottles each. If the product is successful they tell you they would expect to place the same order once a month. The market now shrinks to about $6 million. Again you will be able to sell only to pharmacies which serve upper-income localities. Applying the 10–20 per cent rule again and the market potential now shrinks to about $1 million.

Just having a potential market is not enough; the company must penetrate the market and obtain market share. Again there are some common rules worth remembering. First it is rare for any business to gain more than a one-third market share and it is rare for a product to build up market share at more than 2–3 per cent a year. Thus for our hypothetical bath gel we are probably looking at maximum annual sales of say $250 000 to $300 000 and initial sales of probably $50 000 to $75 000.

Although this analysis may appear curt it is far more thorough than many experts' reports on products that have listed on Australian share markets. The market for a new engine has been defined as all the new cars built in the world when it is really the car manufacturers. The market for a new rapid paint hardener has been described as the industrial paint-users throughout the world, and so on. When defining the size of the market the entrepreneur should try to establish the following equations:

Size of the market in dollars =
  Average purchase size × Number of purchasers

Size of the market in dollars =
  Average purchase price/unit × Number of units

The reason for calculating these two equations is that inconsistencies between the number of buyers, number of units sold, and average cost per purchase will quickly establish themselves in your perception of the market.

Step 3 Establish the growth rate of the market

After verifying the type and size of the market demand, the next step is to establish the market growth rates. The first step is to visit the Australian Bureau of Statistics (ABS), which houses a staggering amount of information. Often the information you need is immediately available. Even if it is not, you can often obtain surrogate information which indicates demand growth or decline. Two useful surrogate indicators are employment in the industry and the amount of imports. If employment in the industry is growing, it is an indicator that the market for that product is growing. Growth in imports may be distorted significantly by changes in the exchange rate, but changes in import statistics do provide a useful indicator of changes in demand growth.

If the ABS is unable to help, other government departments may provide useful data. Both federal and state governments usually have a Department of Industry, which may well have a section head who monitors data or produces reports on the industry you are interested in. Another potential source of information is the Industries Assistance Commission (IAC), a team of economists that studies industries on behalf of the government to establish if the level or form of government assistance should change. Its investigations usually comprise extensive hearings of industry participants. The reports typically begin with a detailed economic analysis of the industry, which can provide useful marketing information.

There are other sources of information besides the government. Most industries have some form of trade association, which can be a useful source of information even if its covert role may be to keep newcomers out. These associations often produce surveys of expectations and provide a monitoring role. They may supply a history of price movements or wage increases. If either of these indicators is moving significantly upward, so may demand. The other source of industry information is the local industry newspaper. Nearly every industry has at least one trade newspaper. (If it does not, starting one may be an excellent entrepreneurial opportunity.) Half an hour with the editor or its best reporter can provide you with a substantial amount of information.

Recently retired senior executives may also provide useful information. They have often gained extensive knowledge about an industry and it has been my experience that they welcome the opportunity to discuss it. Their analyses are usually intelligent and penetrating.

Step 4 Establish whether the buyer trends are favourable

The final stage of this initial analysis is to establish whether the consumer dynamics are favourable. To list all the buyer trends is impossible, but a key to the success of entrepreneurs is their ability to focus on what new things people and organisations will buy.

The demographics of a country are the basis for the demand. Those that characterise Australia during the 1990s are:

- ageing of the population and the shift of the baby bulge to middle age;
- polarisation of wealth and the formation of the new poor based on a combination of unemployment, family separations and early retrenchment;
- increased concern with ethics and conservatism;
- the shift to the sunbelt;
- a concern for the environment;
- a shift towards Asia both as a source of tourists and exports.

Any analysis of people's preferences and expectations is bound to be subjective. Nevertheless writing down the type, size and growth rates of your market, followed by the dynamics of demand and then referring to it later is a key task in any business analysis.

Supply analysis

With supply analysis, the focus changes from the customer to the competition. The first steps in supply analysis are to establish the stage and structure of the industry, the potential for substitute products and the nature of the barriers to entry.

Step 1 Establish the stage of the industry

Each industry goes through a number of phases and the opportunity for entrepreneurs varies with each stage. The first stage is the *establishment stage*, when there is one product with limited variety and the companies making it are small. The industry is generally started by a technical innovation, although occasionally a change in government policy provides an opportunity. Two famous Australian examples would be FM radio and the freight forwarding industry. Another opportunity comes from social changes. Time sharing and investment advice are two examples of industrial opportunity created by social change.

The next stage is the *growth stage*, when companies develop variety in their products and their marketing methods improve. More companies enter the industry and all show good growth independent of their efficiency. The growth stage provides an excellent opportunity for the entrepreneur. Tourism and peronal computers are good examples of growth industries in Australia.

When demand for a product stabilises and the market gradually transforms itself from initial purchase to replacement purchase, the industry reaches the *mature stage*. Competition intensifies and rationalisation occurs as larger companies discover that takeovers of their smaller competitors are the easiest way to increase market share. Until recently, the opportunities for entrepreneurs in mature industries were limited. However, new financing techniques, particularly leveraged buy-outs, have provided a new opportunity for entrepreneurs. Brewing, food, consumer durables and automobiles are all examples of mature industries.

The final stage is the *decline stage,* when an industry's products are superseded by new products or processes, or demand falls because of a change in lifestyle. Sometimes a technological innovation or a change in the price of a substitute product can rejuvenate an industry and provide opportunities for entrepreneurs. A good example of rejuvenation was the coal industry, which was revived by the large increase in the oil price in the 1970s.

Entrepreneurial opportunities exist at each stage of the industry cycle but the growth stage combines the greatest opportunity with the least risk.

Step 2 Establish the structure of the industry

Economists define an industry structure according to the number of supplying companies. The number can range from single suppliers such as Australia Post in the postal industry, to few suppliers such as in the television industry, to many suppliers such as in the advertising industry. Structure is important because it determines the ability of an individual company to set prices. If the number of companies in the market is large, then the company essentially becomes a price taker, concentrating on production costs and trying to establish product differentiation. With some products differentiation is possible, but generally it is limited.

There are few single-supplier industries or monopolies. Monopolies typically occur because of government licensing, either by setting up a public corporation such as Telecom or Australia Post or by the granting of a patent. Xerox and Polaroid are examples of companies which have occupied monopoly positions. Monopoly companies are price makers and typically set the price as high as the market will bear while still able to buy all the goods produced.

Between these two extremes are found most industries in the Australian private sector. One common structure is an industry with few suppliers or dominated by several large companies. Economists define this structure as oligopolistic. Competition can be based either on price or on other factors. The brewing industry provides a good example. In the early 1980s the New South Wales market was subject to heavy discounting until Castlemaine took over Tooheys and Carlton United Breweries took over Tooths. The price war stopped and the competition became non-price as both companies engaged in heavy advertising and established new brands. This shift to non-price competition allowed the entry of boutique breweries.

The other common structure is called monopolistic competition. In this type there are many small units, but each differs in small ways from its competitors. The typical difference is location, although factors not related to price, such as advertising and branding, may affect competition. A good example of monopolistic competition is the photo-finishing industry.

For entrepreneurs structure is important for two reasons. If the competition is non-price, they have the opportunity to create product differentiation, although this may be expensive. On the other hand, if the competition is solely on price and they discover a new form of low-cost production, they will be able to penetrate a market rapidly, as happened in photo-finishing.

Step 3 Establish any potential for substitute products

Most companies have some form of competition. Even in a

monopoly situation, there is the potential for substitute products: For example, electricity has gas as a competitor for heating, synthetic fibres may replace wool and cotton, wine may replace beer. Supply analysis requires consideration of such potentials.

Step 4 Establish the nature of any barriers to entry

It has been suggested that in an oligopolistic structure what the few participating companies fear most is the entry of new companies from other industries or overseas. The entry of new companies will reduce market shares and disturb pricing structures. Hence companies in oligopolistic industries try to set up barriers to entry. In the next chapter, we define how entrepreneurs must establish sustainable competitive advantage. This is equivalent to creating barriers to entry, so to prevent repetition we will simply say here that typical barriers to entry are capital costs of entry, control over distribution outlets or factors of production, brand image and advertising, economies of large-scale production and unavailability of finance.

3 The competitive advantage: why will your business win?

In the previous chapter, we examined ways of deciding on the size of a market. The reasons for this were twofold. First, insufficient size of market is a common reason for business failure. Aspiring entrepreneurs can save much time and money if by dint of analysis they establish that the market is too small to support the business proposal. Second, by analysing a market in the manner proposed, aspiring entrepreneurs should be able to create another necessary criterion for success: a sustainable competitive advantage.

The sustainable competitive advantage is based on what the advertising industry calls USPs, or unique selling propositions. USPs are those unique features of the product that satisfy the customer's buying motives. An example will best explain the concept. Imagine you are a creative writer for an advertising agency and an agricultural marketing board has come in with a new fruit, which they are calling an 'orange'. They give you a dozen of them, along with a dossier on the product, and ask you to devise an advertising campaign. After you have read the dossier and tasted the product you take the first step in any marketing campaign and list the product features:

- citrus fruit
- natural—grows on trees
- contains large amounts of vitamin C
- distinctive taste
- orange colour
- distinctive smell
- can be made into marmalade
- makes a juice
- juice can be fermented and distilled into a liqueur
- product has an impermeable skin
- skin is easily peeled
- product can be segmented

- product contains a self-reproducing mechanism (seed)
- product can be sliced
- skin not easily edible
- skin can be shredded and put into Christmas and other cakes
- spherical shape
- easy to pack into display pyramids
- high fruit to skin ratio
- between skin and fruit is a material called pith, and so on . . .

The next step is to establish what might motivate people to buy it. This list is usually far shorter. The potential reasons for buying the 'orange' appear to be:

- desire for healthy food and drink
- pleasure
- desire to cook cakes, etc.

The next step is to write down the main features of the product that you think customers might be looking for.

Features	Benefit
natural	healthy
citrus fruit	healthy
contains vitamin C	healthy
orange colour	pleasure to the eye
different taste	pleasure to taste
goes into cakes	desire to cook, etc.
makes juice	desire to cook, etc.
makes marmalade	desire to cook, etc.

The next step is to establish if there are any unique selling propositions. As you go down the list, you strike out the following items:

- natural—pears, apples etc are natural
- citrus fruit—lemons and grapefruits are citrus fruits
- contains vitamin C—lemons, grapefruit and limes are sources of vitamin C
- orange colour—tangerines are orange
- makes marmalade—ginger, grapefruit and lemons make marmalade
- makes juice—nearly all fruit can be juiced

Thus at the end of your analysis you establish that the only USP is the taste of the orange. You decide to make taste the focus of your marketing campaign.

This discussion, although hypothetical, has some clear lessons:

- first, all products or services have associated with them a whole host of features;
- second, customers have, by contrast, little motivation to buy;
- third, few USPs can be associated with a given product.

It is the task of the entrepreneur to first recognise a product's USPs and then ensure that the marketing campaign is based on them. Far too many products or services are established with no USPs. Even when USPs exist they are either forgotten or buried under a host of other features.

Product-related USPs that cannot be imitated are the best. The classic situation is a business based on a technical monopoly, such as Polaroid or Xerox. Location is another good USP. Retailers have long been aware that location is often the key competitive edge one shop has over another. Another common USP is price. If because of some manufacturing advantage you have the lowest-priced product, then you have a definite USP.

It is important to try to ensure that the USPs are tangible. A friend of mine once invested in a small snap-printing business located in a side street in the centre of a major city. After several months, sales were flat and going nowhere, and he asked for help. I visited the shop and during the meeting with the management, asked what made their business unique. They replied 'service'. I asked them to quantify service, which they were unable to do. We then carried out the exercise of listing features, motivations and benefits. We concluded that the important USP of the business was two off-street parking spaces, which meant customers and couriers could easily deliver and collect printing jobs. A dodger was printed with this message, distributed and mailed out, and business boomed.

Another technique for developing a USP is to segment a market according to some variable and focus on that segment. One common variable is household income or wealth, another is age of the customer. McDonald's focuses on families with young children, Mercedes on more affluent households. Over time the company develops an image appealing to this market niche.

Complementing the idea of USPs is the economist's concept of barriers to entry. As the market for a product or services develops, a few companies gradually become dominant. It becomes increasingly difficult for new companies to enter the marketplace. The older companies' success builds barriers to entry that newcomers must hurdle. Examples of barriers to entry are:

- *economies of scale*: large-scale plant investment by the incumbent companies means they are the lowest-cost suppliers;
- *blocked distribution channels*: retailers are disinclined to provide shelf space to new companies and prefer successful existing brands. Retailers charge significant fees to carry a new line;
- *advertising:* new entrants have to spend significant sums to obtain any form of brand recognition and the big advertising companies are already handling the incumbents' accounts.
- *reference sales and national service networks:* this can be a significant barrier for new companies targeting the industrial and government markets.

When considering 'why their business will win', entrepreneurs should view the marketplace as a set of scales. In one pan is the business with its USPs and in the other pan is the competition with its barriers to entry. How the scale pointer moves provides some indication of the market share the company could expect to gain.

Thus the next step in analysing business potential is to establish if there is sufficient competitive advantage to get a market share that will provide adequate returns to shareholders. If entrepreneurs are satisfied the business opportunity is there and the competitive advantage can be sustained, they can take the third and final step of financial analysis.

4 The initial financial analysis

Let us assume the prospective business passes the twin tests of sufficient market size and sustainable competitive advantage. The next step is to establish the financial viability and financial requirements of the business.

Business provides rewards in many ways but to attract the institutional investor reward must come in some financial form. Businessmen need capital to establish and operate a business. The capital may be equity, supplier credit, debt or some combination of these. The providers of the capital typically seek a return and this measure, 'the return on capital employed', is the fundamental ratio used to analyse a business.

All businesses may be defined as enterprises that purchase inputs such as labour and materials, add value in some form (usually requiring the purchase of capital equipment), and then sell the transformed inputs. The cycle of buying and selling is then repeated. Businesspeople refer to the buying and selling cycle as the turning over of assets. One key to business success is achieving a greater asset turn than your competitors. One way to calculate asset turn is to divide annual sales by the total assets employed in the business. Another more common way is to subtract current liabilities from total assets and define the result as 'capital employed'. The ratio of annual sales to capital employed is the 'capital turn'. The balance sheet of the company describes how much capital is employed in a business and how it is distributed among the various assets.

In accounting terms:

> Assets = Liabilities

> Long-term assets + Current assets = Current liabilities + Long-term debt + Shareholders' funds

> Long-term assets + Current assets − Current liabilities = Long-term debt + Shareholders' funds

Definitions:

>   Working capital = Current assets − Current liabilities

>   Capital employed = Long-term debt + Shareholders' funds

Thus:

>   Long-term assets + Working capital = Capital employed

Another key to business success is the difference between the purchase price of the inputs and the selling price of the outputs. The profit and loss account is the accounting report businesspeople use to measure this difference. Successful businesses are defined by the profits they achieve. The usual measure is the percentage of annual sales that annual profit represents. This percentage is known as the profit margin.

When the capital turn and the profit margin are multiplied together, they define the return on capital employed:

>   Return on capital employed = Profit/capital employed

>   ROCE = Profit margin × Capital turn

$$= \frac{\text{Profit}}{\text{Sales}} \times \frac{\text{Sales}}{\text{Capital employed}}$$

The target figure of, say, 20 per cent for the pre-tax return on capital employed is the same for the majority of businesses. However, the means by which this target is achieved varies from industry to industry. Oil refineries need extensive capital investment and usually have profit margins of 20–30 per cent and capital turns of 1 or less. On the other hand retail establishments which sell mostly for cash, lease their fixed assets, and whose major asset is stock typically have pre-tax profit margins of 2–3 per cent and capital turns of between 10 and 7.

Once the capital requirements are defined, the next step is to establish the mixture of supplier credit, debt and equity to finance the business. Typically for most businesses supplier credit is the cheapest form of financing, followed by debt, and then equity. The financing task is to try to borrow as much as is possible and top up any deficiency with equity. This is the leveraged buy-out financing technique. The corollary is that because interest payments must be met, debt increases the financial risk of a business. For a start-up business the business risk is already high, so adding financing risk can be too much. Thus, if possible, equity should finance new businesses. Indeed, if entrepreneurs try to raise equity and fail, they are receiving an important message. To neglect this signal and try to fund a start-up with debt is a common mistake, and often leads to bankruptcy.

Returning to the questions set at the beginning of this chapter, the steps to establish the financial viability and financial needs of a business are as follows:

- First draw up a monthly pro forma profit and loss account of the business when it is an on-going business and operating profitably. At this stage the business should be generating positive cash flows.
- Then calculate the gross and pre-tax profit margin ratios and establish whether they are sensible.
- Convert the monthly pro forma profit and loss accounts to annual figures. Then establish the capital-employed ratios for similar industries and calculate the capital requirements for the continuing business.
- Then try to establish how much capital will be needed to fund the business until the business turns from cash negative to cash positive. This should not be longer than two years but is often longer than one year.
- Add the ongoing capital requirements to the start-up capital requirements and then decide if and how you can raise the needed capital.

Let us now take as an example a company that wishes to manufacture a new form of electronic widget. The total market is estimated to be $15–20 million and because of your pricing and technical advantages you believe you will obtain 10–15 per cent of the market in two years.

- You estimate widgets will cost $1500 to make and will sell at an average price of $3000. You estimate that to achieve sales of $180 000 a month the company will need a sales manager and four salesmen. Other necessary staff overheads include an accountant, a research and development engineer, a technician, a secretary and a receptionist.
- You then draw up a monthly pro forma profit and loss account as shown in Table 4.1 and calculate percentages. Note that we are assuming nothing about the method of financing and are supposing there is no interest to be paid. Thus EBIT (Earnings Before Interest and Taxation) is equal to the pre-tax profit. Fixed manufacturing costs refers to

costs such as rent, equipment leases etc., which do not vary with the volume of manufacturing. Cost of goods sold refers to the direct labour and material costs incurred in production.

- You then check the pro forma profit and loss percentages against industry norms and establish whether your projections are realistic. The most important percentage is the profit before tax. More business plans lose credibility with this figure than with any other. Manufacturing enterprises may occasionally exceed 10 per cent but it is rare. Resource-based businesses in good years may achieve 40 per cent but the matching cost is the enormous capital infrastructure which must be built. Few businesses continuously achieve pre-tax margins of more than 15 per cent.
- The next step is to find out the asset turn for an electronics manufacturing business. From your research you find the typical asset turn ratio for an electronics manufacturer is 1.5.
- Thus by calculating the annual sales for the company, $2.16 million, you estimate that its asset requirements would be about $1.4 million. Creditors and leave provisions typically represent 20–25 per cent of total assets, leaving an operating capital requirement of $1.2 million. For a manufacturing company of this size the assets would typically be fixed assets of $500 000; stock of $450 000; debtors of $400 000 and other assets of about $50 000.
- In addition you estimate it will take the company eighteen months to build up sales to $180 000 a month. Thus in the first month the company will make a gross margin of $5000, in the second month $10 000, etc. Over 18 months the total gross margin earned will be $855 000. The monthly fixed cost is estimated as starting at $38 000 and growing to $77 000 at a rate of $2000 a month. Over eighteen months the total costs will be $1 035 000. The difference between the total gross margin and total costs is a capital deficiency of $180 000. The total capital requirement is thus about $1.4 million. The monthly profit before tax is estimated to be $13 000, which leads to an annual pre-tax profit of $156 000 or a return on capital employed of about 11 per cent.

This simple example is at the level required for initial analysis. Perhaps the most common reason given for business failure is undercapitalisation. What undercapitalisation usually

Table 4.1 Monthly profit and loss with percentages

	$	%
Sales	180 000	100
Cost of goods sold	90 000	50
Gross margin	90 000	50
Marketing & sales	40 000	22
Administration	15 000	8
Research & development	10 000	6
Fixed manufacturing	12 000	7
Earnings before interest and taxation (EBIT)	13 000	7

means is that the entrepreneur underestimated the capital requirements.

The key step is the second one, which is drawing up a proforma profit and loss or income statement and calculating the various percentages. Ken Olsen, the founder of the second-largest computer corporation in the word—Digital Equipment Corporation—has said the first question he asks of any aspiring entrepreneur is to see the income statement. He does this before any questions about markets, technologies or previous track record. He says he knows whether the business has any chance of success from the quality of the income statement. If the income statement appears reasonable the next step is to calculate the margins. In a start-up manufacturing company, one usually looks for gross margins over 50 per cent, marketing costs of 20–25 per cent, administration costs of 7–10 per cent, and research and development costs of 5–10 per cent. For a retail or wholesale operation you look for margins of 25 per cent and overheads of around 18 per cent.

Once you have estimated the income statement, the calculation of the capital turn is relatively simple. Typically manufacturers have a ratio of 1.5–2 while retailers, who can sell for cash, lease equipment and premises, and use suppliers' credit, can achieve capital turns of 8–12.

The more difficult task is the calculation of capital needed to fund the business till break-even cash flow is achieved. Each business is different but there are some rough rules of thumb. Most companies require at least a year to start making a profit on a branch operation. Another rule is that for every dollar spent on successful research and development, up to three dollars are needed for production engineering and up to six dollars for the marketing and production launch. Underestimation of the start-up capital is a major risk for most investors, particularly if the investment needs further research and development. Thus a preferred alternative for many entrepreneurs is to take over an existing business; that is the subject of the next chapter.

Of course these calculations are only satisfactory for a first analysis, but they do provide some useful indicators. Any formal fund-raising will need a business plan and detailed monthly cash flow forecasts. Later chapters describe how these reports are prepared, but in the next section we examine the financial intermediaries which can provide debt and equity capital to entrepreneurs.

5 Taking over an existing business

Till now we have been examining the initial analysis necessary for starting a new business. However, while starting a new business and succeeding can bring about some spectacular gains, there are other ways to win, namely turnarounds and leveraged buy-outs.

When entrepreneurs take over failing (or failed) companies and by a combination of innovative marketing and cost-cutting convert the losses into profit, this is called a turnaround. Lee Iacocca of Chrysler and Victor Kiam of Remington are two well-known examples of such entrepreneurs. Their books are well worth reading and are an inspiration to any budding entrepreneur or manager. Turnarounds, however, are notoriously difficult. Successful company doctors, another name for turnaround experts, are as rare as successful artists. Thus, if you are offered a turnaround opportunity, it is necessary to exercise extreme caution and ensure you have developed a business plan for success.

The leveraged buy-out is another method of buying companies, and it has become increasingly popular over the past five years. A leveraged buy-out replaces business risk with financing risk. All businesses are subject to failure; indeed failure is the essence of the capitalist system. Failure redirects resources towards more productive enterprises. Business failure often comes about because the marketplace or competition prevents adequate sales or margins (business risk). In other cases, the business has been financed by too much debt in proportion to equity and because of an economic downturn is unable to meet its interest payments. It is then foreclosed by the debt financiers (financing risk).

Figure 5.1 illustrates the risks facing businesses as a simple grid. Section 1 is a well-managed, successful business. Typically the debt–equity ratio is 50:50. Section 2 is a start-up financed by equity. The business risk for a start-up is always high but the financing risk is small because there is little debt on the balance sheet. Section 3 is a start-up financed by debt. This is usually a disaster. Section 4 is a leveraged buy-out. A company with little business risk and a strong balance sheet is purchased principally by debt financing, generally raising the debt–equity ratio to a maximum of 90:10. The essence of a leveraged buy-out is to weaken a previously strong balance sheet. The reward for the entrepreneur comes from using the cash flows of the business to repay the debt so that in time, the debt–equity ratio declines to about 50:50.

The result, provided the business keeps the same value, is a fivefold increase of the equity. Figure 5.2 illustrates this.

LBOs have become increasingly popular overseas. Financiers and entrepreneurs can now do cash flow analyses on personal computers. Sufficient successful examples of LBOs are available to convince doubtful lenders. Some large LBOs have already been carried out in Australia. The most successful was Kerry Packer's buy-out of Consolidated Press. He bought back from the public the half shareholding his family did not own for $300 million in 1983; sold half the business (the Nine television network) to Alan Bond in 1987 for $1.1 billion; bought that back in 1989 for $200 million; and then in 1992 sold half the magazines (effectively one-quarter of the business) to the public for $600 million.

The success of an LBO, provided the price is right, depends on a steady cash flow. Thus one looks for businesses in quasi-monopoly situations with high barriers to entry. For Consolidated Press television licences were restricted, demand for television advertising generally exceeds supply and the cost of setting up a new newspaper or magazine in the markets already served by its publications was prohibitive. Castlemaine Tooheys, a leveraged buy-out executed by Alan Bond, was in a similar

Figure 5.1 Risks facing businesses

		Financial risk Low	High
High	Business risk	2	3
Low		1	4

Figure 5.2   Increasing equity in an LBO

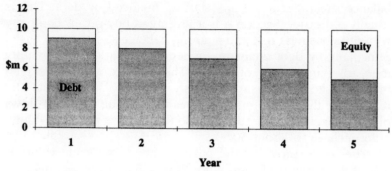

position. The costs of building a large brewery to obtain the necessary economies of scale and the further costs of advertising and significant discounting to achieve high market penetration means breweries are almost impregnable. The last attempt by Courage Breweries to enter the Melbourne beer market was a costly failure.

Consumer businesses that have strong brand names and few competitors are popular targets for LBOs. Other potential candidates are industrial companies that are sole suppliers. A good Australian example is Austoft, formerly known as Versatile Tofts, which is the dominant worldwide supplier of cane-harvesting equipment to the sugar industry.

The first step in an LBO is establishing the size and stability of the market. The second step is to discover the degree of competition. It is critical to establish the potential for price-cutting by competitors. A highly leveraged company cannot afford to engage in a discounting war and is particularly vulnerable to a squeeze on margins.

Finally, the entrepreneur must establish whether the company can refinance the debt from the operating cash flow or asset redeployment. Usually a new emphasis on asset management can reduce stock and debtors, and delaying payment to creditors may significantly reduce the working capital requirements of a company. Some fixed assets, particularly land and buildings, can often be sold and leased back. On a per capita basis, Australia has the largest property trust industry in the world and these institutions are often seeking good properties or tenants.

The principal form of asset redeployment is probably reduction of stock levels. Typical measures carried out by management are:

- doing product rationalisations (long-established companies tend to have an excessive number of low-margin products);
- introducing stock recording and control systems;
- reducing set-up times on machines so the factory can produce on shorter runs.

If entrepreneurs cannot establish a means of financing the debt (if the price is too high), there is no deal.

In this chapter we have concentrated on leveraged buy-outs. However, entrepreneurs can also consider the purchase of a small existing company. The purchase of a small company that already has a number of facilities in place (phone, post office box, etc.) and a developed credit history may often prove to be an intelligent step. Entrepreneurs should remember that the winner of the inaugural 1987 Flying Start Award, DKS Pty Ltd, was founded when shareholders bought a small manufacturing company in 1979 for a five-figure sum. They sold the business to James Hardie in 1991 for an eight-figure sum.

PART II

THE VENTURE
CAPITAL SPECTRUM

6 How the game is played

In Part I we described how entrepreneurs should analyse a business and decide whether it is worth trying to raise funds. In Part II we will examine the various venture capital intermediaries. Before this, however, let us first look at how the entrepreneurship/venture capital game is played.

Not much in the venture capital game is new. What is different is that the game and the roles of the various players have become more precisely defined. The rules for this game developed in California during the 1960s and 1970s. It is only recently that the game has really started in Australia, although it was practised for a time among the junior resource companies in Perth. Significant changes in the Australian financial system over the past ten years have made the entrepreneurship/venture capital game a more popular one to play.

It is worth describing how people used to be able to make money in Australia. Before the changes introduced by Treasurer Paul Keating and the Labor government in the late 1980s, the rules were as follows:

- high inflation because of loose monetary policy;
- no capital gains tax;
- corporate tax rate of 50 per cent;
- no taxation of superannuation;
- double tax on dividends.

That is, not only were company profits taxed at the corporate tax rate, but the dividends declared were further taxed at the marginal tax rate of the recipient. Entrepreneurs would thus use the operating cash flow of a business to pay as much interest and as little tax as possible. The interest would be used to service debt to buy appreciating assets, typically property. To raise money you went to the banks and borrowed. Even listed companies did this, as Statex figures show. (Statex is the information service of the Australian Stock Exchange). The ratio of debt to shareholders' funds rose from 40 per cent in 1980 to nearly 100 per cent in 1989. The ratio of pre-interest cash flow to interest payments dropped from six to three. This investment strategy, known as negative gearing, was practised by companies and individuals alike. Thus the 1980s became known as the decade of debt.

The game has now changed significantly.

Tight monetary policy is causing inflation rates to be low

Few people in Australia have yet realised how a low-inflation environment is going to change investment decisions. A good question to ask is how long it will take a property whose value has fallen by 50 per cent to recover its original value if inflation is running at 4 per cent. The answer is nineteen years. Previously, when inflation was 10 per cent, the answer would have been nine years. The 1980s strategy is less attractive.

Capital gains tax has been introduced

No longer are capital gains tax-free. Now they are taxed at the marginal rate adjusted for inflation. Again the 1980s strategy is less attractive.

The corporate tax rate has been lowered

At the time of writing, the corporate tax rate in Australia has dropped to 39 per cent and accelerated depreciation has been introduced. The global competition for capital investment means it is unlikely that these rates will rise. Lower corporate tax rates reduce the attractiveness of the 1980s strategy of negative gearing.

Taxation of super funds

The institutions represent about 85 per cent of the investment in the Australian share market. They are now taxed at 15 per cent. Previously their preferred strategy was to trade heavily and try to make capital gains. Now, with the introduction of capital gains tax and dividend imputation (see below), their whole investment strategy has changed.

Dividend imputation

Of all the changes that have been introduced in Australia, this is probably the most important. Many people still do not understand how dividend imputation works. Effectively, attached to every $100 of dividends on which corporate tax has been fully paid is $64 in franking credits. Tax-payers who receive these dividends add them to their taxable incomes, calculate the tax to be paid, and then deduct the franking credits to establish the tax payable. Table 6.1 show the calculations for three classes of tax-payer.

The super funds have a tax credit of $39 and can shield a further $39/0.15, or $260, of income from non-franked sources. Already dividend imputation has caused many changes in the investment community. Among the more important were the collapse in the share prices of the non-franked, low dividend-paying companies such as Bond Corp and IEL, and the shortage of stock as institutions hoard fully franked dividend-paying shares. In addition, companies have introduced dividend re-investment schemes, in which the shareholder reinvests the dividend so the company keeps the cash but the shareholder keeps the franking credits. In 1990, for example, the same amount, $2.3 billion, was raised by dividend reinvestment schemes as was raised by rights issues. Also, the owners of profitable companies are now making the companies pay tax and taking the tax-free dividends. Kerry Packer, for example, is not paying a low rate of tax because of tax avoidance, but because nearly all of his income is in the form of fully franked dividends so his marginal tax rate is only 13 per cent.

To quote Paul Keating: 'The dividend imputation system, which removes the double taxation of dividends, changes the balance between equity and debt. In the 1970s and 1980s we were taxing debt once and equity twice and leaving capital

Table 6.1   The operation of dividend imputation

Marginal tax rate	47%	39%	15%
Dividend received	100	100	100
Franking credits	64	64	64
Taxable income	164	164	164
Tax due	77	64	25
Less franking credits	64	64	64
Actual tax paid	13	Nil	(39)

gains tax free; we're now taxing debt once and equity once, and taxing capital gains. *The 1990s will be the decade of equity.*'

Many budding entrepreneurs may find this difficult to believe, but a big problem facing the Australian venture capital community is the lack of good investments. Australia is not alone in this predicament. Venture capitalists in the US had the same difficulty in the late 1960s and early 1970s. However, understanding of how the entrepreneurship/venture capitalist game was played gradually developed. It spread by word of mouth and has now been documented in several books. In this book I have tried to summarise how to play the same game in Australia.

There are many players in the game, but the most important are the entrepreneurs and the venture capitalists.

Venture capitalists in essence are managers of financial intermediaries. Investors subscribe equity capital into a company, trust, or limited partnership. Venture capitalists in turn invest the funds raised in the form of equity in small private companies. The objective is to grow the funds under management. There are two reasons for this:

- the management fee (typically 4 per cent a year) is usually related to the size of assets under management;
- there is usually a performance incentive in the form of a percentage (typically 20 per cent) of the value added to the initial funds raised.

Venture capitalists achieve their return as capital gain. The exit mechanism is generally either by an initial public offering (IPO) or by an acquisition by a larger corporation. Typically they invest in companies with a value of up to $10 million and seek to grow them to valuations of $10–25 million.

To achieve a successful float on the main board of the Australian Stock Exchange a company should have a valuation of at least $20 million. This practical limit is set by the need to have a floor under the share price. To ensure a minimum price a company should have the support of the institutions such as the large insurance companies and pension funds. The institutions prefer to invest in minimum amounts of $1 million and prefer to own less than 5 per cent of a company. If they own a larger amount and wish to sell, the selling program may depress the exit price.

To achieve a valuation of $20 million a new float should

have a history of gradually increasing profits, a profit after tax of $1 million for the year preceding the float and a prospective forecast profit after tax of $1.5–$2 million. Thus what venture capitalists seek are investments in growth companies or in leveraged buy-outs where there is significant potential for growth in equity.

The definition of entrepreneur in the *Concise Oxford Dictionary* is 'a person in effective control of a commercial undertaking'. A better definition of the entrepreneur is a person who converts an idea into things or a service that people buy. Entrepreneurs may do this for many reasons but the successful entrepreneur does it for one underlying reason, and that is to get rich. If the profit motive is not there then a necessary ingredient for success is missing. Note that a desire to get rich is not sufficient. Many of the wheeler-dealers of the 1980s had the desire for wealth in abundance but instead of being entrepreneurs as they claimed, they were arsonists, destroying the companies they acquired.

How are entrepreneurs to become rich? In the 1990s they best fulfil this aim by owning shares in a public company. It is worth analysing some figures provided by the Sydney Stock Exchange. In 1991 there were 1151 companies listed on the Main Board of the Sydney Stock Exchange. Each of these companies has a market capitalisation which is defined as the product of the number of shares on issue and the last traded share price. The market capitalisation is the valuation placed on the company by the market. The total market capitalisation of the Australian share market on 30 June 1991 was $228 billion. The mean average capitalisation of a company listed on the Australian Stock Market was $198 million.

Such a figure is misleading. In Australia the share market is dominated by the 231 companies which make up the All-Ordinaries Index and represent 92 per cent of total market capitalisation. What we should look at is the average figure for the 920 non-Index stocks, which is $19.8 million. An entrepreneur who owns 10 per cent of an average non-Index company thus has a relatively liquid asset of $2 million.

To accomplish the goal of public listing, entrepreneurs have to perform, and the key measure of performance is after-tax profit. The price–earnings ratio (P/E ratio) for the Sydney Stock Exchange on 1 January 1992 was around 15. Thus the average non-Index Australian public company was earning $1.3 million after tax.

The chief constraint on entrepreneurs is the recognition that they should be seeking equity funding rather than debt. Investors think of equity capital as risk capital because they have no guarantee of any return on their investment nor of its repayment. By contrast, debt has a fixed interest and a fixed term over which the money is lent. From the perspective of a business, debt is more risky than equity and financiers use the ratio of debt to equity, known as 'gearing', as a measure of financial risk.

For a new company the business risk is high. Therefore the entrepreneur should minimise the financial risk. The source of funding should thus be equity rather than debt. In the US high-tech companies have little or no debt on the balance sheet.

The chief constraint on venture capitalist is operational. The fees from $5 million will support one venture capitalist and administrative overheads. The maximum number of investments a venture capitalist can manage is around 10, which sets an automatic average funding amount of $500 000 per investment and a minimum amount of around $250 000.

Now we have defined the objectives and constraints, it is necessary to define how the entrepreneurship/venture capital game is played.

Perth has long had the reputation of being the entrepreneurial capital of Australia. Various reasons have been suggested for this. The main industry in Western Australia is mining. If you wish to set up a company for exploration you do not go to the bank for funds. What you try to do is raise equity and the most common way is by small public company listings or private subscription. As the culture of fund-raising by equity develops, the word spreads and more true entrepreneurs appear and use the same fund-raising techniques in other industries. Thus true entrepreneurs flourish in a climate of equity fund-raising. Indeed, the point at which the 'new' Perth entrepreneurs such as Alan Bond and Laurie Connell went off the rails was when they started to finance equity investments with debt.

By contrast, in the other cities of Australia entrepreneurs have traditionally tried to finance start-ups using bank debt. Banks lend money if they are confident that there is the capacity to pay the interest and the collateral to repay the principal if

Table 6.2 **Funding requirements for a high-growth company ($ '000)**

Year	1	2	3	4	5
Sales	100	200	400	800	1600
Profit after tax	10	20	40	80	160
Retained earnings	8	16	32	64	128
Stock	8	16	32	64	128
+ Debtors	16	32	64	128	256
− Creditors	4	8	16	32	64
Working capital requirements	20	40	80	160	320
Less : retained earnings	8	16	32	64	128
Funding requirements	12	24	48	96	192

problems occur. Few start-ups have either characteristic. Thus, there has developed a lack of business-building entrepreneurs.

Indeed, as demonstrated earlier, the taxation structure worked against this. Now the environment has changed. While the 1980s has become known as the decade of debt, the 1990s will be known as the decade of equity.

The venture capital/entrepreneurship game has six rules:

- A rapidly growing business is always short of cash and the over-financed company does not exist.
- Raising cash is done by a series of capital placements which results in continual dilution of earlier investors and founders.
- All the shareholders are driven towards the goal of maximising after-tax profits and an eventual public listing even though they know that if they are successful the greater likelihood (by a factor of four) is takeover by a multinational.
- Entrepreneurs who worry a lot about voting control usually have nothing to worry about.
- There is no limit on what you can do or how far you can go—if you don't mind who gets the credit.
- The probability of success of a small company is inversely proportional to the size of the managing director's office.

Let us examine in Table 6.2 an imaginary company where:

- turnover doubles every year

- there is a gross margin of 50 per cent
- 10 per cent is earned in after-tax profit
- all its fixed assets are leased
- debtors pay 60 days after receipt of invoice
- creditors require payment within 30 days and represent 50 per cent of cost of goods sold
- stock levels are two months of cost of goods sold
- 80 per cent of after-tax profit is retained in the company.

A high-growth business, if successful, goes back to the venture capital market repeatedly to fund the working capital requirements arising out of rapid growth.

Table 6.2 is made more relevant by the following practical example (see Table 6.3), which shows the financing history of a company over a four-year period. The company begins with 1 500 000 $1 shares partly paid to 1 cent. The first venture capital investor puts in $500 000 for 25 per cent of the company.

What happens (as illustrated respectively by Figures 6.1, 6.2 and 6.3) is that funds are raised in stages, the founders' equity is diluted at each stage, and although the percentage holding becomes smaller the real value of the holding becomes greater as the value of the company increases.

This example is important, and all budding entrepreneurs should study it carefully. It demonstrates a number of key principles of the venture capital game:

- The founders and management end up owning 34 per cent of the business; the holding is worth $9 million compared with an original value of $15 000.
- Equity is used to compensate the executives and the employees. Everyone in the company has a vested interest in increasing the value of the company's shares. Profits are not eroded by the executives taking high salaries.
- The fund-raising never stops. The finance director is responsible for raising the next round of equity. Typically in the intervals the finance director arranges debt as bridging finance to cover timing differences.
- The dilution curve for the founders' equity is a hyperbola. While the founders' equity is initially only diluted by the start-up investors, in subsequent rounds the earlier investors share the dilution with the founders.
- The increase in value of the company is a combination of two processes: first, the increase in value generated by the

Table 6.3 Pro-forma financing history of a high-growth company

Stage	Founders issue	Start-up	Round 1	Round 2	Float	Post-float
Month	0	0	12	24	36	48
Issued shares		1 500 000	2 000 000	2 666 000	3 666 000	4 416 000
New shares	1 500 000	500 000	666 000	1 000 000	750 000	
Total shares	1 500 000	2 000 000	2 666 000	3 666 000	4 416 000	4 416 000
Share price	$0.01	$1.00	$1.50	$2.00	$4.00	$10.00
Post-funding valuation	$15 000	$2 000 000	$4 000 000	$7 333 000	$17 666 000	$44 166 000
Funds raised	$15 000	$500 000	$1 000 000	$2 000 000	$3 000 000	$0
Pre-funding valuation	$0	$1 500 000	$3 000 000	$5 333 000	$14 666 000	$44 166 000
Cumulative funds raised	$15 000	$515 000	$1 515 000	$3 515 000	$6 515 000	$6 515 000

Share structure	Shares on issue		Percentage holdings		Value	
	Shares	%	Round 1 %	Round 2 %	%	$
Founders/employees	1 100 000	55.00	41.25	30.00	24.91	11 000 000
Managing director	200 000	10.00	7.50	5.45	4.53	2 000 000
Marketing director	100 000	5.00	3.75	2.73	2.26	1 000 000
Finance director	40 000	2.00	1.50	1.09	0.91	400 000
Operations director	60 000	3.00	2.25	1.64	1.36	600 000
Investors: start-up	500 000	25.00	18.75	13.64	11.32	5 000 000
Round 1	666 667		25.00	18.18	15.09	6 666 000
Round 2	1 000 000			27.27	22.64	10 000 000
Public Float	750 000				16.98	7 500 000
Total	4 416 667	100.00	100.00	100.00	100.00	44 166 670

Figure 6.1   Funds raised in stages

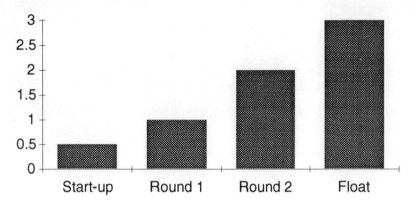

continual increase in profitability, which financial analysts refer to as the 'quality of earnings'; second, the increase in value that comes from the conversion from a private to a publicly listed company. As a rough rule of thumb a company may be valued as follows:

- 1/3 the All-Ordinaries P/E when private;
- 2/3 the All-Ordinaries P/E on listing;
- 100 per cent of the All-Ordinaries P/E after making the forecast profit stated in the prospectus.

• Money invested stays in the company and is used to finance the growth of the business.

Entrepreneurs and investors should also realise at what stages venture capitalists invest. The seminal paper on small business growth is by Churchill and Lewis. In this paper the authors begin by dispelling the myth that companies follow the classic product cycle of start-up, rapid growth and maturity.

Instead they developed their own five-stage model of small business growth:

Stage I: Existence

At start-up a company's strategy is to stay alive. The owner does everything and is the major supplier of energy and direction, and, with relatives and friends, capital. Systems are non-existent. The owner controls the company by watching the bank balance.

Figure 6.2   Dilution of founders' equity

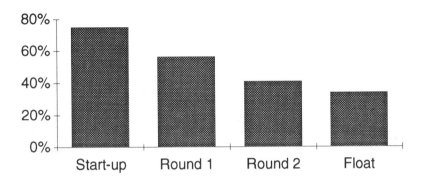

Stage II: Survival

At this stage the company is at marginal profitability. Many 'mum and dad' stores are at this stage. The owners may have some employees and an external accountant. If the company appears to be succeeding it may raise capital from wealthy individuals known as 'angels', or from the public sector, or very occasionally from venture capitalists.

Stage III: Success

The company has succeeded and is showing an economic return on investment. It is generating cash. Professional managers in the form of a financial controller and a production scheduler join the company and basic systems are introduced. The owner then has two choices. He or she can decide to disengage from the business and use the money to finance a pleasant life-style. As outlined earlier, another common strategy in Australia has been to buy property.

The other strategy is to go for growth. In Australia this would mean opening interstate or other branch offices, for example. Now the owner must be deeply involved. He or she can use several different financing strategies. Franchising is a good technique for consumer products, provided the gross margin is large enough. Knitwit is a good example of a well-run franchised operation. The other method is to seek equity from venture capitalists and go the dilution route outlined above.

Figure 6.3   Increasing value of founders' equity

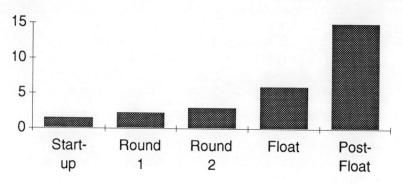

This technique works best with products and services sold to the industrial and government markets.

Stage IV: Take-off

In this stage the company grows rapidly. The two key problems are financing the growth and organising the delegation and decentralisation of responsibility. Two mistakes are common. Often, the owner does not realise that dilution is the name of the game and that the way to protect himself is to ensure a spread of ownership and not let one party control the company. It is at this stage that there are multiple fund-raisings from venture capitalists. The other common mistake is for the owner not to realise that the business and ownership have become separate and that the business is going to need other management resources besides the owner to run the company.

Stage V: Resource maturity

At this stage the company has delegated and decentralised management and formal planning systems in place. The company has arrived. If it can preserve its entrepreneurial spirit it will be a formidable force in the market. It is generating cash and the problems now become ones of diversification.

The point about this model is that it describes the businesses venture capitalists seek. They do not seek companies at Stage I or II. When they do, their successes become the stuff of legend. Digital Equipment Corporation, mentioned earlier, is a case in point. However, for many companies, even those claimed as successes by the venture capitalists, such as Apple in the US and Neverfail Springwater in Australia, the initial start-up financing was done by the entrepreneur and friends, the survival stage was financed by 'angels', and only in the success and take-off stages did the venture capitalists appear.

Neverfail Springwater is a good example of the 1990s growth model in action. In the four years to June 1992, in what could only be called a poor business climate:

- the company grew from nothing to an installed base of 33 000 water coolers;
- the turnover went from nothing to over $20 million a year;
- the total equity capital raised was $12 million and the company was debt free;
- the founder went from 100 per cent to 35 per cent ownership;
- the share price went from $1 to $300;
- the founder's shareholding grew in value from $60 000 to $18 000 000.

It is not just the skill of the management, nor the implementation of the business concept, but the method of financing which has been a key to the success of Neverfail.

The next two chapters examine the sources of start-up and development (second-stage) venture capital financing. Chapter 9 looks at the financing of leveraged buy-outs and also explains how the rules of the LBO game differ.

7 Seed and start-up capital

As indicated in the previous chapter, one essential principle entrepreneurs trying to build a high-growth business must grasp about the venture capital game is that the fund-raising never stops. However, the hardest part is raising seed money. In this chapter we analyse the various sources of seed and start-up equity funding.

The various financing stages are defined as follows:

Seed: financing to start up a company and develop proto-types.

Start-up: financing received before a company makes any sales.

Stage I: seed and start-ups are grouped together as Stage I financing, when the company has no sales and no profits.

Stage II: financing received when a company is making sales but no profits.

Stage III or development: financing received when a company is making sales and profits.

Public-sector funding

A major source of seed and start-up funding is the public sector. In most OECD countries the public sector provides seed finance and no doubt will continue to do so in the future. However, if there is a trend developing in the public sector, it is the recognition that it should switch its funding philosophy from the scattergun approach of funding a multitude of small projects to the large-scale funding of major projects.

Surprisingly, no government has ever formally expressed the reasons for this change in strategy. Nevertheless, the economic reasoning is sound. Since World War II world trade has expanded significantly. Unfortunately for Australia, the segment showing the highest rate of growth has been elaborately transformed manufactures, while the slowest growing segment has been commodities. As the Espie report noted, it is not small companies that provide the elaborately transformed manufactures but rapidly growing companies. Perhaps the best example of such a company would be Nucleus, which makes a wide range of complex medical devices. In other words, to establish a more favourable balance of trade, Australia needs to promote not small business but rapidly growing businesses. If we define a rapidly growing business as one that doubles in turnover every year, then if the first year's turnover is $1 million, the company's sales over a five-year period will total $31 million. Let us assume research and development expenditure is 10 per cent of turnover and the R & D budget is split equally between new products and product enhancement. In addition, if the average product life cycle is five years then the initial R & D funding base for the first product will need to be of the order of $1.5 million.

Before the latest federal government scheme, known as the Discretionary Grants Scheme, was introduced the average R & D grant was around $100 000. Since the introduction of the scheme the average grant amount has approximately tripled. In 1990–91 78 projects were awarded an average of $285 000. Moreover, the federal government has so far targeted five new or emerging high technology areas, namely biotechnology, new materials, information technology, communications technology, and environment technology, for special grants known as Generic Technology Grants. The average grant for the 24 special projects given funding in 1990–91 was more than $500 000. The combined annual total for Discretionary Grants and Generic Technology Grants in 1990–91 exceeded $45 million.

This change in philosophy augurs well for entrepreneurs. Previously the scattergun approach rejected commercial and realistic projects in favour of trying to spread as much money among as many projects as possible. Now entrepreneurs have an excellent opportunity to raise seed funding.

The problems with government funding are threefold. First, annual allocations can mean a twelve-month wait if you miss the cycle. Second, the selection process is lengthy. Finally, the money, as for much government funding, is allocated on a dollar for dollar basis.

Before entrepreneurs lose heart, however, they can raise grant money conditionally. The game then becomes one of interesting other investors conditional on raising Discretionary Grant Scheme money, which is then obtained. Entrepreneurs can then go to the other investors with their Discretionary Grant Scheme money as a bargaining chip. Any proposal which results in doubling of the investors' leverage will have some appeal. To be successful, of course, entrepreneurs require a commercially valid business plan. How to write one is the subject of Part III of this book.

Besides the Discretionary Grant Scheme, the federal government has several other grant and industry assistance programs. Some are directed towards specific industry segments and are often the result of campaign promises made in the heat of an election. For example there are more than twenty agricultural R & D funds. The budgets are large and often unallocated—only $523 000 of the $12.8 million allocated in 1987–88 to the Heavy Engineering Research and Development Scheme was actually used. Other funds are directed towards the development of prototypes to be used within the government. For example Telecom has a $5 million Product Development Fund which has started several businesses and the National Procurement Development Program (NPDP) in 1990–91 allocated $6.3 million to support the development of 23 prototypes to be used within the government. Prototype funding is particularly attractive as the designer develops a product in response to specific market need and should have a first customer to provide an endorsement. Prototype funding provided by the public sector has seeded many high-growth companies in the US. The best known example is Hewlett–Packard. The two founders, after whom the company is named, designed and manufactured in the proverbial garage a device for the electrical engineering department of Stanford University. The company then sold the same device to other universities using Stanford as a reference.

Besides the federal government funding, each state also has several bodies providing funding assistance. For example, New South Wales has a scheme known as FIRST (Funding for Innovation, Research and State Technology) which so far has invested $2.5 million in seed projects.

It is not the purpose of this book to provide a complete list of the various funding sources available. The list would be out of date upon publication. Furthermore, the funding strategy and budget allocations for governments vary annually. There are several excellent government directories available. The best is the *Scitech Technology Directory*, compiled by Jane Ford, the editor of the monthly magazine *Scitech*, and published annually by Scitech Publications Pty Ltd, GPO Box 1915, Canberra, ACT 2601.

The federal and state governments have set up in each state a central source of information called the National Industry Extension Service (NIES). NIES is a good first contact point as it keeps an up-to-date government assistance directory. The local state office is well worth a visit by any entrepreneur. NIES also provides financial and other support for the development of business plans—typically the funding is provided on a dollar for dollar basis. In 1990–91 more than 1450 Australian companies received some form of financial assistance from NIES.

There are many consultants who specialise in raising money from government bodies. The good consultant charges on a success-only basis and typical rates, depending on the funds raised, are between 3 per cent and 5 per cent. A consultant can be most useful, providing he is wired into the network; the only way to find out is to establish his track record. Good consultants should be able to screen your proposal and provide realistic counsel on the potential for fund-raising. They should have good lobbying contacts and be able to advise on the preparation of grant applications. The local NIES office should be able to supply a register of suitable consultants.

The latest initiative of the government for Stage I funding was announced in the February 1992 Economic Statement. This is the formation of the Australian Technology Group (ATG), which is to have a one-off capital base of $30 million. The ATG is to identify research with commercial potential and if necessary provide seed capital to bring it to a stage where it would be attractive to private sector partners.

Private sector institutional funding

Another source of funding is the private venture capital companies. As a general rule these companies prefer second stage funding but do allocate part of their portfolios to seed and start-up fundings.

One group of private venture capital companies is the

Management and Investment Companies. The MIC program, introduced in 1984 by the federal government to encourage the development of a venture capital industry, was terminated in June 1991. The MICs were to provide financial and managerial support to innovative technology enterprises that had the potential to grow rapidly and help the balance of trade. The model for the program was the successful Small Business Investment Corporation program (SBIC) which has been running in the US since 1958. The principal recipients of MIC support were to be start-up and early growth companies. However, over time the portfolio emphasis shifted to early growth and development businesses. Individual MICs are covered in the next chapter.

The MIC program had two components: the allocation of approved capital and the licensing and monitoring of the MIC companies. Approved capital was the amount of capital MICs were entitled to raise from investors, who in turn were allowed to claim a 100 per cent tax deduction. Few people realise the original fund-raising in 1984 got off to a rocky start. This was because the primary source of investment in Australia, the pension funds, were not taxed. A 100 per cent tax deduction was of no advantage while retail investors could obtain a better tax break (133 per cent) from film investment. Only two-thirds of the amount licensed was raised by June 30, 1984, which meant that afterwards the MIC companies, instead of dealing with the investment proposals which were flooding in, were still trying to raise funds.

The MIC's fund-raising efforts met with greater success until the sharemarket crash of October 1987 effectively eliminated the retail investors from the market. The majority of superfunds, even though they had become taxable entities, refused to invest in MICs, for being 15 per cent taxpayers they did not find the tax deduction very attractive. Only when the MIC board permitted the MICs to raise funds in the form of convertible redeemable preference shares—which effectively gave the investors a 100 per cent tax deduction on capital subscribed, the certainty of regaining all the capital invested in four years, and a free option—did the MIC fund-raising efforts again meet with success.

The MIC program, however, has been and will continue to be an important source of venture capital. During the life of the program $392 million was raised for investment. So far more than $150 million has been invested in 155 different businesses.

While the investment flow has declined considerably from the heady days of 1986–87, when over $53 million was invested in 47 businesses, capital is still available. There has already been some rationalisation among the MICs, with several being managed by others. While new funds will no longer be raised, MICs will be divesting from businesses and looking for new investments.

Fourteen MICs were eventually licensed by the board. There is no doubt the program was adversely affected by the 1987 crash, which severely dented retail investor confidence and caused professional institutional investors to seek 'blue-chip' stocks. In the Australian equity markets there was a flight to quality. However, the loss of favour of venture capital was also dramatic overseas, as Table 7.1 demonstrates. It is also worth noting the difference in the amount of venture capital raised on a per head of population basis. Australia is disproportionately low.

While there is no doubt that the investment climate adversely affected the MICs, the licensing strategy of the MIC board compounded the problem. Any licensing board always has the dilemma of building a market versus supporting inefficient competitors. This is because licences will, if the supply is restricted, have some element of monopoly value. The original licensees argue strongly against the allocation of further licences and by persistent lobbying 'capture' the licensing agency. In Australia the airline industry has been a good example of agency capture.

There are three ways of avoiding agency capture. One is to start by licensing so many participants that the monopoly value of the licence is negligible. The federal government did this most successfully when it licensed 40 foreign exchange dealers instead of the expected ten, and sixteen foreign banks instead

Table 7.1   A comparison of overseas and MIC fund-raising efforts

Country	1987–88	1988–89	% decline	1988–89 per captia
Australia MIC	$A40.78m	$A15.73m	61%	$A1
US	$US4.9b	$US2.9b	41%	$A15
UK	£UK708m	£UK700	1%	$A25
Canada	$C800m	$C475m	41%	$A21

of the expected six. The second method is to provide the licences automatically if certain criteria are met, of which the most important is a capital base. This is how the SBIC program operates in the US. Provided a company has an original $5 million equity capital subscribed it can then apply for an SBIC licence. The SBIC can then borrow up to a limit at favourable rates of interest for later investment in small companies. Over 600 SBICs have been licensed of which 200 have failed. Nevertheless the other 400 have been the training ground of the US venture capital industry. The third method is to make sure monitoring after the initial grant of the licence is slight and new licences are easy to obtain. This is the method adopted by the Bank of England, which takes a liberal and market-driven attitude towards the granting and subsequent monitoring of banking licences in the United Kingdom.

Unfortunately the MIC board, which contained no economists, adopted the opposite approach. The criticisms of the MIC program were the usual criticisms of any industry where the barriers to entry are high and the original players have captured the entity. The MIC board covertly changed its charter from developing an industry to trying to protect the original licensees. This gave the MICs a non-competitive, insulated air. For the first four years the board appeared to restrict the number of licences to eleven and allocate most of the tax-free capital to the original members. What it should have done is allocate four new licences a year of $10 million each and tell the new licensees that after the initial allocation they were on their own. Four new licensees each year would have kept the other participants competitive and perhaps led to the program continuing.

In the February 1992 Economic Statement the government announced a new initiative—Pooled Development Funds (PDFs), which are meant to replace the MICs. As these entities are precluded from investing more than 5 per cent of total funds under management in Stage I companies, they will be covered in Chapter 8.

Private sector non-institutional funding

This is probably the largest source of funds for seed and start-ups both in Australia and overseas. It involves friends and relatives or wealthy individuals known as 'angels'. This is an unorganised market which depends on networks of accountants, lawyers and stockbrokers. The major change that has occurred in this market was the introduction in January 1991 of the new prospectus regulations.

Before January 1991 there was always the question whether, when entrepreneurs went seeking equity funds, they were breaking the law. Under the Companies Code only if a person was seeking money from the public was it necessary to register a prospectus. Who were 'the public' was a moot point. For example, an offer to 38 000 members of a credit union was ruled by the courts not to be an offer to the public.

Under the new Corporations Law the rules are far less ambiguous. A prospectus must be registered unless there is a relevant exception. This is not the place to list all the exceptions but the key ones for entrepreneurs are:

- an offer of at least $500 000 in one lot. It does not matter if the investor takes up a smaller amount but the expectation must be that the offer will be accepted for the minimum amount
- an offer to an investor controlling net assets of at least $10 million
- an offer to executive officers, their relatives, and family companies
- an offer made to no more than 20 persons in the previous 12 months.

With these four exemptions, it is unlikely that any entrepreneur who wishes to play the entrepreneur/venture capital game of Chapter 6 need worry about having to register a prospectus. On the other hand entrepreneurs should still follow in their business plan the main precepts of all prospectuses now being issued. These by law shall:

> contain all such information as their investors and private advisers would reasonably require, and reasonably expect to find in the prospectus, for the purpose of making an informed assessment of:
>
> (a) the assets and liabilities, financial position, profits and losses, and prospects of the corporation; and
> (b) the rights attaching to the securities.

Thus entrepreneurs can form a company, prepare a business plan, and go out and seek money from private investors and venture capital companies without fear of legal retribution.

The other method of trying to raise seed and start-up money is by registering a prospectus, and raising the money with the promise of listing the company. This was the *raison d'être* of the second boards. The second board is the collective term used to describe the separate 'second board markets' which accompanied all the major Australian Stock Exchanges until June 1992. The first second board opened in Perth in July 1984 and at the peak more than 400 companies were listed on second boards. Second board stocks differed from main board stocks in the following ways:

- Lower minimum capital subscriptions
- Lower minimum number of shareholders.
- Differential voting rights attached to shares.

Main board companies tend to follow the principle of 'one share, one vote'. The Stock Exchange Listing Committee has occasionally allowed sliding scales. If a shareholder holds more than 5 per cent of a company the number of shares required per vote increases. For example a shareholder might only get one vote for every 10 shares held over 5 per cent. On the whole the committee has rejected requests by the managements of aspiring main board companies for differential voting rights. New entrepreneurs, who are naturally worried about losing control if the business grows and is successful, seek mechanisms to maintain power. The second boards alleviated this fear by allowing differential voting rights.

After a bright start the second boards are now in the process of being removed. The major reason given was the miserable turnover since October 1987—negotiability is a prime reason for listing on the stock market. However there are a number of reasons why the second boards, and in a sense the whole approach of listing a start-up company on a stock market, are doomed to failure.

The first difficulty is cost. To produce a prospectus a company needs a sponsoring broker, underwriters, investigating accountants, independent experts, and a solicitor. Under the new prospectus requirements these individuals, along with the directors and executive officers of the company, are liable for any misrepresentations or misinformation in the prospectus. Therefore all must carry out extensive due diligence. All these advisers want fees, documents must be printed, and listing and share registry fees must be paid. The fees for a small start-up company could be as much as 12 per cent of the funds raised. Fund-raising fees are capital costs and cannot be written off in the year of fund-raising. Besides the initial costs, publicly listed companies also face the ongoing costs of listing fees, stricter financial reporting requirements and continuous disclosure.

Another problem is the volatility in share prices caused by instability in the share register. Institutions prefer not to support small capitalised companies if they have no earnings history. As a general rule institutions prefer to invest in amounts greater than $500 000 and keep holdings to less than 5 per cent of a company. This leads to a minimum capitalisation of $10 million, which is greater than the capital subscription of many start-ups. The share prices of small companies tend to fluctuate more wildly than those of older, more established companies.

The fluctuating share price creates a significant problem if it falls below the par value of the share and the company needs to raise further equity capital. By law a company may not issue shares below par value. If the trading price of the shares is below par value then a rights issue as a source of funding is unavailable. Some shareholders may take up shares at a pre-mium to the trading price but they are typically a small minority. One solution to this potential problem is initially to issue shares at a premium to par value, but this is difficult for a start-up. Otherwise, if equity fund-raising is the only route, the company must try a private placement. The price charged may be onerous in terms of the share options which must be offered. This is the problem many of the second board companies unsuccessfully faced and a reason why, in general, companies should not list unless they have developed a history of growth in earnings and will be valued at a minimum of $10 million on listing.

Conclusion

The total amount of seed and start-up capital available in Australia probably exceeds $300 million a year. For a country with as small a population as ours, this is considerable. The providers of the capital regard their biggest problem as finding suitable investments. Section III describes how to access this supply of venture capital, but in the next chapter we consider the sources of second stage financing.

8 Development capital

In this chapter we examine the significant sources of expansion finance. Expansion finance is the generic term for second stage and development financing. A second stage company is one making sales and losses while development financing is provided to a company making sales and profits. Again, funding is available from many sources. This chapter adopts the same format as Chapter 7, discussing public sector funding first followed by private sector funding.

Public sector funding

The most popular source of federal funding is the Export Market Development Grants Scheme (EMDG). Using the EMDG, companies recoup expenditure made to promote exports. Companies are entitled to recoup 50 per cent of eligible expenditure up to a maximum of $250 000 for the first two years. After two years the maximum grant is the lower of $250 000 or a percentage of export earnings. The proportion of eligible expenditure falls from 40 per cent of total exports in the third year to 5 per cent in the seventh and successive years. Claims must be for expenditure over $30 000 in one year but smaller amounts may be carried forward and no more than eight claims may be made. The maximum export turnover for which claims may be made is $25 million.

Many rapidly growing companies will have some export sales. By the beginning of 1992, monthly Australian exports were running at around $4.5 billion. The EMDG scheme is a useful source of funds. What the entrepreneur should do is carefully time the first expenditure to ensure maximum recoupment. The maximum expenditure which can be recouped in the first year is $250 000. Typically a US office will cost about $500 000 to set up and it will take about a year before sales start. Hence, as the Australian financial year runs from the beginning of July to the end of June, it makes sense to begin operations midway through the financial year. The enterprise should then be able to recoup start-up costs over two fiscal years. The other major source of trade funding is the International Trade Enhancement Scheme (ITES) operated by Austrade. This scheme will provide up to $2.25 million over two to three years repayable either in the form of a royalty on sales or a low-interest loan. Applicants must show the project has the potential to earn substantial net foreign exhange, which is taken to be at least $20 million over five years.

Another important federal government funding body is AIDC Ltd, which is the privatised form of the old Australian Industry Development Corporation. AIDC was the first government privatisation and the majority of the stock, 81.9 per cent, is still owned by the government. AIDC Ltd has two divisions: Development Investment, which is an equity portfolio comprising 40 investments worth $257 million, and Development Financing, which deals with loans and has a portfolio size of $3.2 billion. The AIDC has made a number of successful large venture capital investments including Southern Aluminium, supplier of aluminium wheels to many of the major car-makers of the world, and Hospital Corporation Australia, which is Australia's largest private hospital company. While it has recently invested in several large seed fundings, especially those which involve partnerships comprising universities, public sector research organisations and private sector companies, much of its funding has been second stage. It also tends to be a large-scale investor and prefers investments of $2 million plus. It appears to be becoming highly selective, making only three new investments in 1990–91.

Another source of government funding is the Commonwealth Development Bank (CDB), which again is a privatised body majority-owned by the government. The CDB can now invest equity as well as provide loan finance. The investments so far have been few and are likely to be so in the future. It prefers maximum participations of up to $1 million.

Most of the state governments have moved from being enthusiastic investors of venture capital to disinterest. The massive write-offs of the Victorian Economic Development Corporation and the West Australian Development Corporation have probably ensured that state public sector involvement as venture capital investors will be restrained. Only Queensland and Tasmania have active state-backed funds seeking investments.

Technology parks are another state government initiative, which may in the long run turn out to be more visible than useful. The most famous is the technology park in Adelaide but Queensland, Tasmania, Western Australia, and the Australian Capital Territory have all been imitators. In the US sociologists have observed that the two largest high technology clusters are next to universities. Silicon Valley is between Stanford and the University of California; Route 128 circumscribes Harvard and the Massachusetts Institute of Technology. One may debate the causality in this correlation, but the correlation alone was seen as a justification for technology parks. The state governments have set up parks with modern buildings and offer rent holidays to attract new enterprises. The jury is still out on whether the technology parks will be a success. While the universities may provide skilled labour, there is a danger of regarding universities as all the same. Most people would include the four American institutions named above in any list of the top ten universities. Moreover, it is doubtful if one could name another group of four universities that would offer as many Nobel Prize winners. In addition these four are all richly endowed and have a long tradition of funding prototypes. Hewlett–Packard, DEC and Wang are examples of companies whose first sales came from producing prototypes for universities. Silicon Valley and Route 128 also have other significant advantages. Boston and San Francisco are significant financial centres; both cities would have larger funding bases than either Sydney or Melbourne. Both areas also have access to inexpensive labour—Silicon Valley has Mexican immigrants while New England had a large pool of unemployed workers from the closure of the original New England textile factories.

On the other hand there is no doubt that some Australian research and development is of world class, two examples being the bionic ear and Enterovax, the genetically engineered oral vaccine developed at the University of Adelaide. The opportunities are available for perspicacious entrepreneurs to access funding to commercialise research and development.

Private sector funding

While the public sector is a source of second stage funding, it is mainly as debt. Similar comments apply to the private sector but equity is also available.

The obvious sources of debt funding are the trading banks and finance companies, which, provided they have security, will generally lend. Sometimes entrepreneurs complain when seeking funding from banks or finance companies because they must provide either security or guarantees. They ask why security is necessary when the banks have so much money. They forget that, while the banks do have money, it is nearly all in the form of deposits; only a small part of the total assets of a bank is equity. Surprising as it may seem, most banks and finance companies are equity short. Indeed, one reason why the banks are on lower price earnings multiples than most other industrial companies is the threat of recurrent rights issues. For example, banks make most of their profit on the interest spread between the funds they borrow and the funds they lend, less administration costs. The actual profit on total assets is less than 1 per cent, so retained earnings build up slowly. The regulatory authorities require every $100 of deposits to be supported by a specific amount of equity. A common prudential ratio for a bank is $1 of equity to support $12.50 of debt. By writing off a bad debt, the banks not only lose equity, but also suffer an opportunity cost by having to reduce debt levels by $12.50 for each $1 of bad debt. Consequently, banks usually adopt a policy of equity retention by means of low dividend pay-outs to shareholders and few, if any, venture capital investments. Sometimes, as happened in the late 1980s, when the Australian government ran a lax monetary policy and allowed explosive credit growth, this policy is ignored. Then, when the bubble bursts, the bad debt write-offs become significant.

Apart from the banks, another source of 'debt funding' is supplier's credit. Retailers and wholesalers have known this for years and many a business has funded itself by stretching out payments to suppliers and obtaining cash from customers. Overseas suppliers, especially those trying to build market share, are often able to offer generous payment terms. These terms are often available because of a loan guarantee supplied by a government trying to encourage exports or by a government body set up to encourage exports. Austrade, the Australian

Trade Commission, provides guarantees to lending institutions which finance Australian exporters. Austrade also provides loans directly to overseas borrowers for the purchase of Australian products.

However, while debt funding and creditors are important components of the financing of any company, what is important to entrepreneurs are the sources of equity capital. The sources of start-up capital listed in the preceding chapter are also sources of second stage and development funding. There are also several private venture capital institutions that specialise in providing development funding.

The largest of the expansion stage institutions is BLE Capital (BLEC), formerly known as Business Loans and Equity Capital Ltd. BLEC is a joint venture between Westpac, AMP and the UK based Investors In Industry (3I). BLEC typically adopts a hands-off role towards investee companies. As a general rule a BLEC investment is unsecured debt (say $1 000 000) with an equity kicker, either taken up for a nominal amount or as options. By the end of 1991 BLEC had provided more than $200 million in long-term debt and equity capital to over 300 businesses in Australia. The present portfolio comprises $160 million invested across 179 companies. On the evidence so far, the company tends to seek between 25 per cent and 35 per cent, tends to work to a maximum investment of $3 million, prefers manufacturing companies, and aims at investing $40 million a year.

The Macquarie Investment Trust is probably the next largest independent fund. It is managed by the Macquarie Bank and has $50 million under management.

A major source of private sector development funding are the MICs. While the program has officially lapsed, a number of MICs have survived to become significant investors. Among the more important are:

Continental Venture Capital

This is the largest MIC, with total assets of $117 million. However, of the $124 million of issued capital $72 million is in the form of convertible four-year redeemable preference shares, which became the only instrument that MICs could use to raise money. Hence CVC can safely invest only the interest from the $72 million it has raised in this form and not the capital. The most famous investment of CVC is Amman Aviation, which won a coastwatching contract from the federal government that was suddenly terminated. Amman sued and eventually won damages worth $9 million.

Hambro Grantham

This group now manages more than $60 million. The former MIC, First MIC Ltd, has been renamed Hambro-Grantham Capital Ltd. It has shareholders' equity of $45 million and a portfolio of sixteen investments. The outstanding success has been the defence communications company Stanilite Pacific Ltd. The original investment of $1 million is now valued at $6.7 million. The other major fund is H-G Ventures, which has shareholders' equity of $11 million and specialises in medical services and health-care products.

Investment Management Associates Group

This Melbourne-based group manages three former MICs: CP Ventures, Austech Ventures, and the Japan–Australian Venture Fund. The group has had some clear financial successes including Clean Line Systems, where a $2 million exposure was converted into $4 million clear profit after costs in 18 months.

The Advent Management Group

This group manages two former MICs, Australian Pacific Technology and Western Pacific, and two other funds, Advent Western Pacific and the Advent Tourism Development Fund. The group is based in Melbourne and is linked to the Advent International Network which was developed by TA Associates, one of the largest venture capital groups in the world. Total funds under management are approximately $75 million. The group's outstanding investment has been Vision Systems, where an equity investment of just under $2 million is now worth $18 million.

The next major sources of funds in the private sector describe themselves as the MIC parallel funds. The Technology Development Trust, Advent Western Pacific, and H-G Ventures are examples of parallel funds. The managers of the MICs formed these companies to raise funds from institutional investors. Nearly all these parallel companies stressed an investment philosophy of development-funding MIC investments and sought also to invest in companies that were ineligible under the MIC guidelines.

Another group of funding institutions are the 'cashbox companies'. These may be regarded as the development funding equivalent of the second board. During the stock market boom and especially in 1986 and the first half of 1987 more than 50 companies were listed with the intention either to invest or acquire other companies or assets. Total funds raised exceeded $500 million. Many of the companies raised amounts which some would consider inadequate to support a sufficiently diversified venture capital portfolio. On the other hand, many of these companies are now seeking businesses in which to invest. In addition, several investment institutions have followed the example of BLEC and have set up venture capital arms with the stated aim of investing in private companies.

In June 1992 the Labor government legislated a new vehicle to replace the MIC program which expired in June 1991. These are the Pooled Development Funds or PDFs. The PDFs have been given certain advantages:

- income of PDFs will be taxed at 30 per cent;
- distributions of dividends from PDFs will be tax exempt, or have franking credits attached through the imputation system; and
- capital gains on the disposal of PDF shares will be tax exempt.

In return the PDFs will have to comply with a number of criteria. They

- must be companies;
- may only invest in newly issued shares in companies having total assets less than $30 million;
- may not invest more than 20 per cent of their funds in any one business;
- may not take up less than 10 per cent of each investee business;
- may not invest more than 5 per cent in start-up businesses; and
- may not invest in retailing operations and real estate other than tourism projects or industrial buildings used by an investee in a manufacturing project.

Figure 8.1   Growth of private venture capital industry

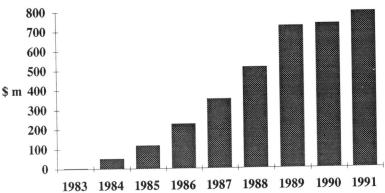

Conclusion

The growth in the private venture capital industry is best shown by Figure 8.1, taken from the 1990–91 MIC annual report. The growth until 1989 was quite impressive. Probably more than $750 million second stage funding and development funding is now either invested or available for investment. This works out to around $50 per head of population. By comparison, the figures for the US and Canada are $250 and $150 respectively. The merchant banks, stockbrokers, large accounting organisations, major law firms, and the NIES databases can all provide entrepreneurs with introductions to potential investors.

9 Funding for management buy-outs

We have now examined two of the three major types of venture capital funding. Seed and start-up venture capital is funding for companies which have neither sales nor profits. Development venture capital is funding for companies which have sales but whose profits could grow significantly. The third kind of venture capital is for those companies whose sales and profits are stable, and which are targets for a buy-out.

There are two classes of buy-outs. The first type is when the current management organises the purchase of the business from the owners and takes a substantial equity participation in the company. The best known and most successful buy-out is Kerry Packer's purchase in 1983, for $300 million, of the 50 per cent of Australian Consolidated Press his family did not control. He eventually sold half the business (the Nine television network) to Alan Bond for $1.1 billion and then bought it back two years later for $200 million. A leveraged buy-out classically occurs when the purchaser is an independent party. Clutha and Castlemaine Tooheys are two of the better-known Australian leveraged buy-outs. The basic financial structure is similar. The cash flow of a target company is used to service and repay debt secured on the assets of the company. Debt to equity ratios of 10:1 are common for buy-outs compared with the financial norm of 1:1.

Given that the target has a history of steady cash flow, the future cash flow is reliable, and the management team is strong, the next task is to try to finance the deal. The first requirement is to carry out an audit of the assets of the enterprise and establish how much secured financing could reasonably be raised. Within the lending industry several rules of thumb have developed about the amount lent on the assets provided.

Property and debtors are regarded as the safest assets and accordingly one can borrow up to 75 to 80 per cent of asset value. This ratio will vary according to the quality of the asset. Debtors' ledgers which are riddled with bad debts and contain large clients with poor credit ratings will be regarded as poor collateral. So will a poorly located factory. Stock and plant are less safe assets and most lenders have had the bitter experience of the monetary results of a stock or equipment auction. Consequently these assets will often secure lending facilities of only up to 50 per cent of book value. Stock which has a low turnover may secure less debt. Similarly, equipment with a limited resale market will have lower collateral value.

Besides the value of the assets, the other key to obtaining secured lending is to demonstrate how the loan principal will be repaid. Banks and merchant banks are the usual sources of secured debt and banks in particular want to see principal repayments in any debt servicing plan. On the other hand, while merchant banks will consider roll-over financing, the interest charged usually means merchant bank financing is the earliest to be paid off.

Secured lenders often will want additional charges over the personal assets of the managers or shareholder guarantees. This requirement should not be necessary for an ongoing business. Fortunately the deregulation of the finance sector has led to increased competition and astute entrepreneurs should be able to find a lending institution willing to lend yet not seeking extra collateral. If entrepreneurs are unable to find an institution, the fault probably lies more with the deal itself than with the lender.

The next step is to establish how much equity the managers can invest. The difference between the consideration required by the seller and the sum of the secured lending and managers' equity is the financing gap. If the financing gap is zero or negative the deal can go ahead, otherwise unsecured lenders and equity from institutions must cover the difference. This financing is known as mezzanine financing because it ranks between the upper levels of debt and the bottom floor of equity in the unfortunate event of a liquidation.

There are now several players in the Australian mezzanine finance market, drawn in by a combination of increased sophistication (using spreadsheets on personal computers) and knowledge of the profits earned by mezzanine financing overseas. Moreover, several buy-out companies and funds such as Byvest, H-G Ventures, BZW Development Capital and DBSM specialise in providing mezzanine financing. BLE Capital and AIDC Ltd are also major providers of buy-out finance. The best directory of mezzanine financiers is the book *Management Buy-outs in Australia and New Zealand* by Ross Grant and David Saunders of Byvest. Any entrepreneur contemplating a buy-out will find this book an excellent reference.

The financing instrument used by mezzanine financiers typically is a hybrid debt/equity instrument. The usual instruments are either subordinated debt with options, convertible notes or convertible redeemable preference shares. All these instruments are described in Chapter 19.

Besides the mezzanine financiers there are other providers of funds. One key provider of finance is the vendor, who may abstain from providing equity but will often provide debt. The provision of a seller's note can often be structured as a discount security, which means the interest payment is made at the same time as the principal is due. The valuation often determines whether vendor finance is provided. If the valuation agreed is less than book value and the vendor must take a loss it will be a persuasive entrepreneur who can then induce the vendor to provide finance. On the other hand, vendors who do not take a loss on the sale will be much more amenable to providing vendor finance.

The other source of funds is the business itself. Typically one aims at a 5 to 10 per cent reduction in working capital as the managers realise it is their money at stake. Asset sales (formerly called asset stripping but now called asset redeployment), especially in real estate, have been a common source of funds, as is sale and leaseback of property. The collapses of the property market and the property trust industry in Australia have made sales and leasebacks far more difficult to achieve.

While buy-outs have yet to reach the same degree of prominence as overseas, there are some financial institutions willing to accept the risk of unsecured lending provided the reward (typically a 35–40 per cent pre-tax return) is available. As the numbers are large—a minimum buy-out should be around $30 million—and there are many players involved in the deal, entrepreneurs almost certainly will need an independent financial adviser.

It should be realised that buy-outs in Australia are subject to higher business risk than overseas. Indeed, several overseas multinational banks, such as Citicorp and Security Pacific, which had encouraged their Australian merchant banking subsidiaries to enter this market, have now withdrawn. There are several reasons for this. First the Australian market is small. The essence of the buy-out market can be thought of as moving companies back and forth across the listed/unlisted boundary depending on the investment climate. The ideal target is a non-core division of a listed company, which is purchased and, after significant debt is paid off, re-listed. To do this you need companies which have a minimum turnover of around $50 million. There are not many organisations of that size in Australia.

Business markets in Australia are fickle. The underlying strength of the Australian economy is commodities, and as the price and demand for commodities vary so does the economy and the demand for other products and services. Turnover is far more volatile than overseas and fixed costs are hard to reduce because of the industrial relations system and the comparatively heavy burden of government charges.

Finally the financial system in Australia is volatile. Interest rates are more variable than in most other OECD countries. Buy-outs which rely on stability to work successfully have had mixed results in Australia. Some have been successful but there have been a number of well-publicised failures.

PART III

RAISING THE MONEY—WHAT ENTREPRENEURS MUST DO

10 How to write a business plan

In the following seven chapters we outline the various steps entrepreneurs must take to raise funds. As suggested earlier, the preferred method is to raise equity from venture capitalists and other sources. Thus in this section we will concentrate on this fund-raising method in our choice of examples and techniques. Nevertheless, the principles and advice provided are equally applicable to other sources of funds such as banks and finance companies.

Essential to success is a formal business plan. There are some legendary examples of entrepreneurs who raised funds without a written plan, but these are the exception rather than the rule. The following chapters provide considerable advice on the content of a business plan, but in this chapter we shall focus on generalities.

The first question is, Who should write the business plan? The answer is simple: the entrepreneur and his or her team. The business plan is the demonstrable proof of how thoroughly entrepreneurs understand their business. If they cannot write about the business, it is unlikely they will be able to run it. Successful entrepreneurs are usually good communicators in writing.

Many companies and individuals offer a consultancy service for the preparation of business plans. Some can be useful for checking figures or doing research. However, entrepreneurs should not use consultants to write a plan.

Preparing a business plan is not simple and is often neglected. The procrastination is often due to deficiencies of the business concept. In an oral presentation it is easy to work up an idealistic fervour. However, the oral presentation should be regarded as a sketch—the business plan stands as the finished product. It is easier to talk about a concept than to write about it. Lack of a plan usually indicates some combination of lack of drive, inadequate business experience, or poor business concept.

A business plan is more than a method of raising funds or separating entrepreneurial wheat from chaff. It is the blueprint for building the business. Just as it would be folly to renovate a house without architectural drawings, so an investor would be foolish to invest in a business without a formal business plan.

The business plan's role as a blueprint transcends its use as a fund-raising document. Anyone who has renovated or built a house knows the first plan is usually different from the finished product. When the concept is down on paper it is easier to change and improve. A plan will go through several modifications. Even more important, it may demonstrate the impracticality of the concept. It is disappointing to prepare a business plan and later conclude the business idea is weak. But the disappointment is minor compared with the pain and anguish which results from a failed business enterprise.

Today's entrepreneurs have a big advantage over those of just ten years ago in access to personal computers. Personal computers have probably cut down the task of producing a business plan by a factor of three to four. Word processing programs, particularly those supplied with spelling and grammar checkers, help entrepreneurs to produce clear, typewritten prose with no spelling errors. Spreadsheet programs are another useful tool for producing financial projections of cash flows, profit and loss statements and balance sheets.

A business plan is not just a prospectus or information memorandum. For those readers unfamiliar with the terms, a prospectus is the formal document used to raise funds from public non-professional investors. It is a typeset document that must be registered with the Australian Securities Commission. Companies wishing to go public, finance companies raising funds via debentures, and unit trusts seeking subscriptions from the public are organisations that prepare prospectuses. Information memoranda are similar documents, used when raising funds from professional investors. Word processors are used for information memoranda but the documents are of good quality. They are typically prepared for institutional fund-raising by private placement or for financing projects. A prospectus or information memorandum is not a business plan. However, a business plan used to raise money from professional investors is an information memorandum.

While the business plan should not just be a device for raising funds, whether the plan raises funds or not is a good measure of its potential success. It is the key selling document for getting a foot through the door of the venture capitalist. Typical venture capitalists probably receive about three business plans a week. They rarely read them for the first time at the office. They are more likely to scan them while commuting or at home in the evening. Thus if entrepreneurs want their business plan read they should keep it under about 40 pages and ensure it will fit into a briefcase. If not, the plan will sit in the pending tray for several weeks until guilt finally forces the venture capitalist to spend ten minutes skimming the contents and writing the rejection letter.

One of the most important sections of the business plan is the executive summary. This section should be written last but have the most time spent on it. (Many business plans conform to the saying attributed to Oscar Wilde: 'I have written you a long letter because I did not have the time to write you a short one.') The executive summary should probably be rewritten six or seven times. The first paragraph is crucial and the first sentence critical. Just as in an advertisement, the first sentence of the executive summary must grab the reader's attention.

The executive summary needs to contain the salient points of the business but three sections are fundamental: the concept, the objectives and the deal.

The concept, sometimes called the mission statement, defines the business in terms of what is to be bought, by whom, and why. Theodore Levitt, in a paper entitled 'Marketing Myopia' published in 1960, illustrated the importance of defining the business mission. He provided two now-famous examples—the railroad industry, which declined because management failed to realise its customers were buying transport, and the movie industry, which slumped until management understood its customers were buying entertainment. The managing director of a large Australian chemical company which had just completed a three-year period of sustained growth was asked for the secret of his success. He replied: 'I spent the first three months talking to management, customers, suppliers and employees working out what we did. I then spent the next three months agreeing with management a 25-word mission statement for our business, which made no reference to chemicals. The next two and a half years I spent reminding the management and employees of the jointly prepared mission statement.' Without a mission statement business can muddle through but it can rarely sustain a high rate of growth.

The objectives should be twofold: financial and personal. Financial objectives are simple. They comprise the target figures for sales, profits and returns on investment. Personal objectives are equally important. Far too often the founders of the business realise too late that their personal objectives conflict with the needs of the business. In the end, much of the capital accumulated by these businesses has ended up in the bank accounts of lawyers. If one founder wants to reinvest the capital to grow the business while another wants a high income to pursue an expensive lifestyle, then it is better to resolve the conflict now rather than later.

Finally, the executive summary must specify the deal. Valuations and structures are discussed in subsequent chapters. The executive summary should at least state the funding requirements and on what basis the investors are expected to invest. The deal will change during negotiation but it can save much time if the investor understands the entrepreneur's expectations.

No two business plans have the same structure but they have certain segments in common. In the marketing segment there is typically a ten-page market analysis section. This should be followed by a five-page market strategy section which defines how the product is to be sold. The next segment should contain operational information. Typically there should be sections on people, management structure, corporate ownership, product development, product ownership, and manufacturing. Overall this segment should contain fifteen to twenty pages. Finally, there is the financial segment, which contains summaries of the cash flow projections.

Once the business plan is completed, the entrepreneur should ask several associates who work in the business to read and criticise it. The feedback should be invaluable. The key questions to ask are whether they would invest in the concept, and if not, why not? If the reply is negative then the entrepreneur must seriously reconsider continuing. The entrepreneur should either forget the project or try licensing the product or process. Budding entrepreneurs should realise that for most inventions licensing is the preferred alternative. While the potential reward is lower, the risks and time spent are far less.

The frequent complaint of inventors that licensees do not take up their invention is usually a result of the inventors' wishful thinking rather than reality. The pressure of competition usually means that if an invention or process does have a chance of commercial success it will be tried. One only has to look at the statistics (where over 95 per cent of products launched fail in the market place) to realise that companies must often be enthusiastic about new products.

Before proceeding to the chapters on market analysis and strategy, operational issues and financial analysis, we will first consider the types of business structures available and the steps required to form a company. While this may appear to be putting the cart before the horse, the appropriate capital structure is a key decision, and takes time to implement. Formation of the company should be done in parallel with the preparation of the business plan and when completed will provide a useful bargaining tool when negotiating with investors.

11 Choosing the appropriate structure

In modern society, the public sector represents perhaps 40 per cent of a country's gross national product. Besides acting as a major consumer of goods and services supplied by the private sector, the public sector interacts with the private sector by making laws and regulations. The legal environment in which a business operates may be divided into two broad categories: *statute law*—which are the laws made by the federal and state parliaments; and *common law*—which represents the decisions made by judges and followed by others to the extent that they become generally accepted practice.

While businesspeople cannot hope to become experts in commercial law, they need to develop a working knowledge of it. The more businesspeople know about the laws and regulations, the more effectively they can manage their businesses. Moreover, they can avoid the costs and time involved in legal action, which can cripple the operation of a business. Fortunately, many booklets and courses are now available for businesspeople to learn about the legal process without paying large fees.

Under common law, of particular importance is the law of contract, especially with customers, suppliers and employees. Under statute law the most important Acts are the Income Tax Act, Trade Practices Act, the Intellectual Property Protection Acts (e.g., patents, copyright, designs, trademarks), and the Corporations Act. There are also the various acts empowering government departments to apply regulations on the use of premises, hours of trading, safety and fire precautions, electrical installations, use of weights and measures, etc.

It is not the purpose of this book to provide an introduction to business law. On the other hand there is one area of law where the entrepreneur and venture capitalist do interact—the ownership and control of business enterprises.

Figure 11.1 Business structures

No separate entity	Separate entity
Sole trader	Trading trust
Partnership	Limited company

A small business may operate in one of four ways, of which two need a separate legal entity. Figure 11.1 illustrates this. The sole trader is the simplest structure to set up and run. A sole trader is only suitable for a small business and not for an enterprise that intends to grow rapidly.

Partnerships too do not involve a separate legal entity. A partnership is defined as a relationship between two or more persons carrying on a business with a common view to making profits. Partnerships can become large—for example, the bigger accounting and legal firms operating as partnerships in Australia employ up to 1000 people. Partnerships have one major draw- back for investors, namely the joint and several unlimited lia- bility on all partners for a firm's debts and obligations. An investor who invests under the aegis of a partnership has an individual liability for the debts of the partnership and the actions of the other partners, and can be personally sued for the liability of the partnership. Litigants tend to sue the richest partner. Even if there is a formal partnership agreement, which restricts the number of partners able to incur debts, it may be insufficient protection and if litigants are unaware of the restric- tion they may sue the other partners for recovery.

The advantage to investors in a partnership is that they will be able to claim any losses made by the investment as a tax deduction by treating the loss as an expense against other forms of income. However, investment in a partnership will limit the potential for capital gains because of the small market for selling a share of a partnership. As indicated earlier, the object of the venture capital game is to accumulate wealth by capital gain; so a partnership structure is the wrong structure because it severely restricts the potential capital gain. It is also an unsound structure because investors will often invest on the basis of an expected income tax deduction during the start-up period.

Thus the question becomes which of the two separate legal

entities to choose: the trading trust or the limited company.
While a book could be written on the pros and cons of either
structure, tax considerations (ironically) affect the choice. Until
the mid 1980s the trading trust structure was the preferred
option. A typical trust structure is shown in Figure 11.2.

A trading trust paid no income tax provided all the income
passed to the beneficiaries. The beneficiaries would then pay
income tax on any income received. The trustee company
would operate on a nominal profit basis covering expenses out
of the trust income and have paid-up capital of $2. If the trust
went into receivership, the creditors would have no recourse
against the assets of the beneficiaries. The creditors would have
recourse against the assets of the trust and could also move
against the trustee. The action would generally gain $2. How-
ever directors of a trustee company are jointly and severally
liable for claims made by creditors if there are insufficient assets,
unless the contracts between trustees and the creditor deliber-
ately exclude the liability. The inclusion of such clauses makes
it difficult to gain reasonable credit from suppliers.

The company structure, illustrated by Figure 11.3, is simpler
than the structure of the trading trust. Effectively, the founders
subscribe for shares in a new legal entity and become directors
of that company. The company is liable for any debts incurred
and upon liquidation the shareholders' maximum loss is their
shareholding.

Creditors do not have recourse to these personal assets of
shareholders or directors unless they can establish either fraud
or negligence. This concept of liability being limited to the

Figure 11.2 Trading trust structure

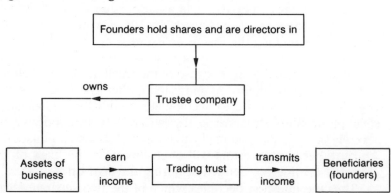

Figure 11.3 Company structure

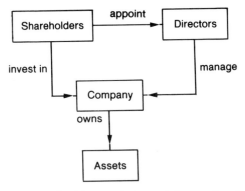

subscriptions of shareholders originated in England during the eighteenth century and was a primary reason for the entrepreneurial explosion which occurred during the Victorian era.

Until recently the problem of double taxation negated the benefit of limited liability. Companies paid a tax on profits, company tax, at a rate of between 40 and 50 per cent. What remained could then be either retained in the company or distributed as dividends. The recipient of the dividends then paid tax at their marginal rate of taxation. Private unlisted companies faced a further complication that if they retained profits above a certain level (even for the justifiable reason of funding further expansion) they had to pay an additional undistributed profits tax. It would be difficult to devise a taxation regime more likely to inhibit economic growth. Economic growth is endogenously generated by either population growth or increases in productivity. One cause of productivity growth is the technological innovation developed and introduced into the economy by new companies. If the taxation environment restricts new companies from adopting new technologies the economy will grow at a correspondingly slower rate.

The introduction of dividend imputation and the taxation of profits made by public trading trusts at corporate rates has now significantly reversed the anti-company bias of the taxation system. With these legislative changes, among the most important introduced by the Labor government, corporate profits are now effectively taxed only once. Dividends received by shareholders on which Australian company tax has been levied are known as franked dividends. Shareholders, who receive franked dividends and whose marginal tax rate is the same as the company tax rate, do not pay any further tax on the franked portion. Indeed those shareholders whose marginal rate of taxation is below the corporate rate will receive a tax credit.

Dividend imputation has received much coverage in the media. The taxation treatment of the beneficiaries of trading trusts has had limited discussion. Company tax now applies to trading trusts but the two structures operate under different taxation regimes. Companies pay tax in arrears while trading trusts operate under provisional tax arrangements.

Provisional tax is an attempt to collect tax revenue in the year the profits are earned. The tax is now paid quarterly and can be a substantial cash flow drain on an expanding business. By comparison, companies pay tax on profits earned in the preceding year. Hence, companies operate under a more attractive tax regime than trusts do. Companies effectively delay cash payments to the tax office by over a year.

Trading trusts share several benefits with companies, largely in the areas of superannuation and the ability to pay fringe benefits tax by the simpler formula method rather than by itemised substantiation. However there are several other taxation benefits that accrue only to companies. One is the 150 per cent research and development tax deduction (see Table 11.1). Under present legislation, R&D expenditure which normally may be charged against income only as a normal expense may for tax calculations be charged at 150 per cent. This can significantly increase post-tax profits.

The other advantage for companies is the availability of group tax relief. Previously, holding companies could not offset

Table 11.1   The 150% R & D tax deduction

Normal deduction		150% deduction	
Sales	100	Sales	100
Other expenses	80	Other expenses	80
R&D	10	R&D	10
		150% adjustment	5
Profits before tax	10	Taxable profit	5
Tax	4	Tax	2
Profit after tax	**6**	**Profit after tax**	**8**

Note: Profit after tax increases by 33%.

the losses in one subsidiary with the profits of another. Losses could offset future profits made by that subsidiary but not profits made by other subsidiaries. As companies grow, they tend to segregate various operating functions into separate companies for management accounting reasons. The ability to offset inter-company profits and losses is a major benefit of the corporate structure.

Finally, taxing public trading trusts has now removed their prime reason for existence. If the goal of the venture capital game is to publicly list, then the trading trust has become the wrong structure.

The current taxation environment now firmly supports setting up a company. The questions then become how and what type. Effectively there are two types of companies: first, *proprietary companies,* which cannot offer their shares to the public. Proprietary companies require a minimum of two shareholders and directors and allow up a maximum of 50 shareholders. Second, *public companies,* which may sell their shares to the public. They require a minimum of five shareholders, two directors and a company secretary and have no upper limit on the number of shareholders. While all listed companies are public companies, a public company is not necessarily listed. As stated before, the objective of the venture capital game should be to create a listed company.

While it is possible to later convert a private company to a public company, entrepreneurs who wish to play the venture capital game should start with a public company. The administration is perhaps more onerous and name changes take longer to execute (which is one reason for starting on the task earlier rather than later), but the later savings are immeasurable. To convert a private company to a public company requires changes to the Articles of Association, which in turn requires shareholders' meetings. If you have already managed to attract several venture capitalists, they will all hire their legal firms to analyse the changes—at your cost. Incorporating these changes earlier avoids costs and delays.

There are two basic documents that detail the way a company operates:

- The Memorandum of Association, which sets out the objects for which the company is formed, its name and capital structure.

- The Articles of Association, which set out the rules for running the company.

The Memorandum defines the capital structure. The minimum size par value share which may be listed on the stock market is 20c, so choose 20c as the par value. Also, entrepreneurs should make the share capital large enough for future growth, say a million shares. In addition, the company will also almost certainly be issuing redeemable preference shares, so it is advisable to set up, say, 10 classes of redeemable preference shares defined as 'A', 'B', 'C' Class, etc., of 20c par value and one thousand in number in each class.

The Articles of Association are important and need close scrutiny. The articles should allow rapid calling of shareholders' and directors' meetings; implementing share issues, transfers and sales by ordinary resolutions; and the use of modern methods of communication.

The simplest way to set up a public company is to buy one 'off the shelf'. Most of the larger legal firms located in the city will have a shelf company available for around $800.

Once you have set up or purchased your company, several key issues must be addressed, namely:

- how much share capital should be subscribed;
- the appointment of directors; and
- the appointment of a company secretary.

The issue of initial share capital is important because it gives a clear sign to investors of how much you as an entrepreneur are willing to risk. It is possible to set up a public company with five shares of 20c each or an issued capital of $1. Most companies have an issued capital of $2, being two $1 shares. Thus one way of distinguishing your balance sheet from other companies' is to subscribe capital. If you go to an investor with a balance sheet that contains, say, $20 000 of subscribed share capital, he or she will treat it far more seriously than a proposal based on a company with $2 of issued capital.

The choice of directors is important because it provides entrepreneurs with one of their few opportunities to independently test their business plan and gain credibility for their proposal. Promoters of public companies are aware of the importance of a reputable board and spend much time choosing the appropriate independent directors. For entrepreneurs the same opportunities are available. An important initial task of the entrepreneur is to recruit a chairperson who is independent, commercially experienced and will provide credibility. The chairperson should provide independent questioning and advice, and not be merely a supporter, as this will dissipate the motivation and enthusiasm so necessary in a business start-up.

The other key appointment is the company secretary. In time, this should be an employee of the company but at the beginning one possibility might be to use a lawyer as a trade-off for a directorship. As this chapter has tried to point out, the law plays a large part in the operation of a company. The person charged with the responsibility of ensuring the company is meeting its legal requirements is the company secretary. Unfortunately this role is often underestimated. Before investing, venture capitalists will require the company to be in complete compliance with the Corporations Code. Among the areas they will scrutinise are:

- filings with the Corporate Affairs Commission;
- issuing of shares and the share register;
- quality of the minutes of shareholders' meetings and board reports; and
- quality and timeliness of the seal register.

The company secretary, besides ensuring the company is meeting its legal requirements, also plays an important role when disagreements occur among founders and investors. The timing, calling and recording of various board and shareholder meetings are all controlled by the company secretary. Another advantage of the company structure is that when things go amiss there is a considerable body of statute and common law to protect the rights of shareholders.

This chapter recommends that entrepreneurs adopt the public company structure as preparation for public listing. The ultimate financial benefits outweigh the administrative costs. Although the company structure restricts entrepreneurs' freedom compared with, say, a partnership, they will usually appoint themselves the directors of the company. The Articles of Association list the directors' powers. However, legislation requires that shareholders meet at regular intervals and for certain decisions, such as appointing directors and setting directors' fees.

The law also places quite onerous duties on directors to act for the benefit of the company. They have a general responsibility to avoid conflicts of interest and must declare personal interests in transactions which might involve the company. Directors must also certify that the company keeps proper accounting records. At the beginning it is usually necessary to hire an outside accountant but the task should become an internal function as soon as possible.

Creditors do not have recourse to directors for debt. However, the law states that directors are personally liable and subject to criminal penalty where they allow the company to incur debts of which repayment is unlikely. Lending institutions will frequently require directors' personal guarantees before lending to the company. Introducing substantial equity into the company is a method of removing the need for these guarantees.

Forming a public company is a key task in raising equity. Another key task is preparing a business plan. The next three chapters deal with this task.

12 Preparing a business plan: market analysis and market strategy

The March 1887 edition of *Scientific American* contained the following passage:

> Inventors often complain of the difficulty experienced in inducing capitalists to join them in their enterprises. Not infrequently the blame rests as much with the inventor as with the man of money. The capitalist is often blamed for not seeing into the advantages of an enterprise, when the fact is it has never been presented to him in the right light. Every man, therefore, who would seek the aid of capital in furthering his plans for introducing an invention should first be prepared to show the whole state of the art covered by such an invention, and wherein the improvement lies. Second, he should, if possible, show what particular market needs to be supplied with such improvements, and something approximating to the returns which reasonably may be expected. Third, he should have some well settled plan of introducing the new product or furthering the new scheme. If his invention is worth pushing, in nine cases out of ten there will be little trouble in procuring financial help if the proper methods be employed.

It is doubtful if better advice on how to prepare a business plan has since been given. A key to the successful business plan is separating the market analysis from the market strategy. In Chapter 2 we demonstrated the technique of analysing a market. We analysed the demand for the product and then we analysed the supply—separately. These techniques for analysing a market may also be applied to the business plan; instead of screening we use the techniques to develop a strategy. If the results of the screening are positive then the market analysis section of a business plan will contain answers to the questions posed in Chapter 2.

In this chapter we will first discuss several extra techniques for market analysis.

Market analysis

The two techniques which should be included in any business plan are customer decision analysis and competitive analysis.

A fundamental question for any business is deciding who really is the customer for the product. Customer decision analysis consists of establishing the purchase dynamics of the product. These are the answers to the famous questions posed by Rudyard Kipling:

> Six true and faithful friends have I;
> What, Where, How, When, Who and Why?

In other words, entrepreneurs find the answers to the following questions:

- Who will make the decision to purchase?
- What are the decision criteria?
- Where is the product bought?
- How is the product bought?
- When is the product bought?
- Why is the product bought?

Entrepreneurs may establish the answers in two ways: by using their imagination or by going into the field, arranging meetings with ten to twenty potential buyers and asking them the questions listed above. The latter course is preferable as it provides some tangible data. It may also provide some prospects for a product. Furthermore, entrepreneurs can also gather data about the competition in order to prepare a formal competitive analysis.

Successful entrepreneurs are aware of their need to stay in touch with the market. They know the best way is to meet face-to-face with prospective and actual customers. Even in the largest companies, the successful executives are the ones who get into the offices of their customers. What applies to successful entrepreneurs applies even more to potential entrepreneurs. They must go into the field early and talk about the product to prospective customers. After each meeting with a customer the first task is to write up notes. If possible you should tape-record the meeting.

It has long been known that researchers unconsciously seek out data that supports their hypotheses. Consequently, good scientists try to set up experiments to disprove a favourite theory. Entrepreneurs must approach market research the same way. They must be careful not just to seek information in support of a new product and reject information that indicates possible failure.

When interviewing prospective customers, entrepreneurs need to be careful. Their passion for a product will often blinker them from any negative reaction from the market. They must provide a calmly optimistic description, which allows the prospect to react. If the prospect's reaction is not enthusiastic within five to ten minutes, there is cause for concern. In the last 50 years we have seen many new products introduced: colour television, video cassette recorders, personal computers, facsimile machines and so on. The market response has been enthusiastic and immediate. I have also been associated with the launch of several product successes and even more product failures. The successes did not take long to build up momentum. Word of mouth seemed to ensure their success or failure.

The data collected from the field should be written up and summarised. The summary should be part of the business plan. The individual reports of the meetings should be kept in a separate file and handed over only if requested. On the other hand, if entrepreneurs do obtain an enthusiastic response from prospective customers they should seek to crystallise the enthusiasm with a formal endorsement on company notepaper. Such endorsements are most valuable and are among the most useful documents start-up entrepreneurs can provide as part of a business plan.

Besides customers there are many other people who can provide useful information about a market and how it operates. As mentioned earlier, I have found the most useful to be:

- ex-executives in the industry;
- editors of trade journals;
- advertising agencies who have run campaigns for the product;
- government advisory bodies for the industry; and
- university professors.

Another important technique is competitive analysis. All businesses face competition—even government monopolies. A distinguishing characteristic of successful businesspeople is their realistic appraisal of their competitive strengths and weaknesses and the development of a competitive strategy. While there are

Figure 12.1 Competitive analysis

Name of competitor			
Estimated market share			
Estimated yearly sales			
Pricing policy			
Advertising/promotion strategy			
Distribution policy			
Service			
Selling force			
Major strength			
Major weakness			
Product life cycle			

many different ways of analysing competition, a method that I have found both easy and effective is illustrated in Figure 12.1—simply fill in the required information. There are several sources that can be used to complete the chart. Facts on the individual companies can be obtained from the Corporate Affairs Commission or credit agencies such as Dun & Bradstreet. Product brochures and newspaper searches are another source of information.

In the majority of Australian business plans, little if any attention is paid to the competition. Omitting any reference to the competition probably does more to damage the credibility of a business plan than any other action. Including a short, realistic analysis and then using the analysis to develop a competitive business strategy provides a good indication of management capabilities.

While the chart begins with some suggested quantitative information, it is not necessary to be precise. Big organisations in stagnant markets may spend hundreds of thousands of dollars establishing market share to 0.1 per cent; such research is a luxury unavailable to the small and growing company.

Far more important is to establish a qualitative feel for the market and the competition. What entrepreneurs need to do is establish the pricing, promotional and distributional strategies of the competition and then try to identify their various market positions.

Deciding on a positioning strategy is the first and most important step in developing a marketing strategy. Positioning refers to a company's placing itself along certain axes by which it defines the market. Occasionally a new product may be introduced to the market; incorporated in its positioning strategy will be a new dimension on which the competition will be positioned. A good example of this is the car industry.

At one time Ford dominated the motor industry with a market share of more than 80 per cent. General Motors, under the new leadership of Arthur Sloane, then developed a new positioning strategy introducing driver status. Against each of the models in the Ford range, General Motors positioned a slightly more expensive car fitted with some extra options to increase the status of the model. The strategy worked very successfully, and General Motors became the market leader. In the 1970s, as rising oil prices forced consumers to reconsider cost, the Japanese introduced the new dimension of value-for-money. In a similar way, Volvo created a new dimension of safety and positioned itself at the top end.

Once the positioning strategy is established, the other components of a competitive marketing strategy, namely pricing, distribution, promotion and packaging, follow.

Marketing strategy

There are three basic marketing strategies that a company may adopt:

- be the low-cost supplier;
- develop a unique selling proposition; and
- focus on a market segment.

The lowest-cost supplier is a market position available to only a few companies. If a company is the low-cost supplier to an

Figure 12.2 The learning curve

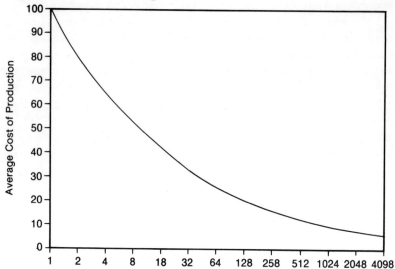

industry it has a strong, sustainable, competitive advantage. Typically the cost advantage comes from economies of scale.

Economies of scale refer to the ability of a large-scale manufacturer, particularly if it has considerable investment in capital equipment, to produce goods at a lower unit cost than a small manufacturer. Examples in Australia are brewing, aluminium and electricity production. For a small, growing company a competitive advantage created by economies of scale is unlikely. However, there is a competitive advantage that can be derived from being first in an industry; it is known as riding the learning curve.

The learning curve refers to a discovery made in the aircraft industry during the 1950s. The cost accountants noted as a general rule of thumb that for each doubling of the production run the average unit cost of production over the total run fell by 20 per cent. Figure 12.2 shows the learning curve effect for a hypothetical product with an initial unit cost of $100. After about 4096 items are produced the average cost of production has dropped to around $10 and the marginal cost (the actual cost to produce the 4097th item) is even lower.

The learning curve has been shown to operate across a wide range of industries. The best-known recent example is the semiconductor industry. A company launches a new design that becomes popular and then rides down the learning curve ahead of the competition.

Developing a technically based USP is probably the most useful marketing strategy of the high-tech business. If by research and development a company can provide a product in the market place with a genuine use, then it can acquire a large market. Examples in Australia of such development are rare. One is the titanium pacemaker developed by Nucleus, but more prosaic examples include the Monier roof tile and the Westfield shopping centre. A USP need not just be a technical advantage; market leadership may also be generated by company positioning. One famous technique is to choose an unusual colour— Farley Lewis distinguished its cement from other cement by painting its trucks pink.

The final strategy is to focus on a market segment. By simply generating a new variable or concentrating on a particular segment of the market a company can gradually establish a market position. The retail market abounds with examples of market niches developed by a focused marketing strategy. McDonald's, Just Jeans and Knitwit are all examples of organisations whose initial marketing strategy was to focus on a product or a particular segment of a market.

Pricing

After the positioning and marketing strategy, the next key decision is pricing. Pricing separates the successful businesses from the failures. The secret to pricing is to first analyse the competition and establish the range of prices, from lowest to highest. Pricing then becomes a question of solving the equation.

Price (new product or service) =
Price (lowest of competition) + F (price range)

The value of the factor F can be estimated in a number of ways but the simplest method is to list, rank and weight all the features in the market place and then score your product on a range of one to ten. F is then the weighted average mean of the various features expressed as a percentage. For example let us assume that you wish to introduce a new car to the family market. You might rank the features as illustrated in the first

Table 12.1   Pricing a new product

	Ranking	Maximum score	Product score	Weight
Fuel economy	10	10	5	50
Safety	9	10	6	54
4 doors	8	10	0	0
Power steering	6	10	10	60
Automatic	4	10	3	12
Power windows	2	10	0	0
Total		**390**		**176**

column of Table 12.1. You would then score your product against the competition as in the third column. The weight in the fourth column is the product of the first and third columns. Here, $F = (176/390) = 45\%$.

Pricing in this fashion could justly be regarded as an artificial calculation. On the other hand it introduces systematic analysis into the pricing calculation.

Pricing policy should also address:

- add-ons
- up-rates
- discounts
- rent rolls.

Add-ons refer to supplementary charges that can be justifiably added on without causing grief or embarrassment. Add-on charges are an economical way of adding to profit. Companies that have been in existence for a long time have generally developed several add-on charges. A good example would be the supplementary charges banks add on to a loan besides the standard interest charge. These charges can add substantially to the total interest bill. As you are intending to establish a company that will be in existence for some time, developing a range of add-on charges is excellent policy.

Up-rating refers to a method by which the pricing schedule is changed to reflect inflation, changes in costs, discounting by competitors, etc. Pricing is probably the most important marketing factor after positioning but usually receives insufficient attention. One of the best lessons I ever learned about business concerned a division of a large freight-forwarding multinational which had just slipped into loss-making. It was decided to hold a management conference to agree on remedial policies to restore profits. The managers gave their individual presentations on how this could be done. The state managers wanted money for more salespeople, the marketing manager wanted more money for promotion, the operations manager wanted new trucks, the administration manager wanted a new computer, and so on. After about six hours the managing director of the company, who is one of Australia's most successful businesspeople, stood up, after having said nothing all day. He turned to the general manager, asked how much freight was carried a week, and received the answer, '4000 tonnes'. He then looked at the budget and said that the weekly budgeted profit shortfall was $8000. He suggested adding on $2 a tonne to the price and walked out. The decision was implemented and profits were restored. What the MD knew was that while the price sensitivity of new customers is high, once a prospect is a regular customer, price sensitivity lessens. Successful businesspeople adjust their price schedules accordingly.

The other key aspect of pricing is discounting. In the computer industry it is said 'You do not have your first site until you have your first sale; but you cannot get your first sale till you have your first site.' This maxim refers to the need for a reference or demonstration site for capital goods or service marketing. A common strategy for many companies is to set up and staff a demonstration site. This is a mistake. Big companies can afford high marketing costs; small, growing companies cannot. What the small company must do is discount. It is important that the discount is understood to be a one-off, special, never to be repeated offer. Entrepreneurs must gain from their initial clients as many non-financial benefits as possible, particularly reference visits.

To quote the example of the freight forwarding division again, when the company opened a new route it would discount to marginal cost and load up the first truck with new business. It would then start to up-rate and replace any lost business with new business at the new up-rated price. The salespeople would no longer focus on discounts but on service, reliability and satisfied customers. When the first truck was earning adequate profits a new truck would be introduced and the process repeated.

The final aspect of pricing policy is establishing a rent roll.

What entrepreneurs want is for the business to make money while they sleep. They want to establish a steady cash flow rather than rely on one-off sales. Consumer items that wear out, such as razor blades and ballpoint pens (53 million ballpoint pens are sold in Australia each year!), maintenance contracts, and management fees are all examples of steady cash flow. Warehouse pallets are a good example of an average business converted into spectacular returns by introducing a weekly hiring policy. It is even better if the regular income is linked to the consumer price index (CPI). A good example is maintenance contracts for computer equipment, which start as an annual charge of 10–20 per cent of the purchase price and rise with the CPI. Over a five-year period the client usually pays more for maintenance than the initial purchase price.

Packaging

Packaging is becoming an increasingly important part of the marketing mix. As the cost of sales staff and media advertising continues to rise, and the retailing and wholesaling industries continue to move to self-service supermarkets, packaging is becoming the silent salesperson. Packaging is the last part of the marketing mix a prospect sees before he or she makes a purchase decision. Industries such as alcohol and tobacco, which have government restrictions on advertising, are spending increasing amounts on packaging. Industrial products are also making increasing use of sophisticated design and packaging concepts. An example familiar to many people is the gradual increase in quality of the manuals for computer software. In the beginning the manuals were often photocopies stapled together. Now they are sophisticated publications which may cost over $100 000 to write and produce.

Re-packaging or a packaging difference may create a USP for a product which results in a telling competitive advantage. DBase is the top selling database software for personal computers. It achieved its dominant position by innovative packaging. It was sold in a shrink-sealed wrapper with a sample system on a separate disk. Prospective users, on payment of the package price, were given both the sample disk and the system disk with the guarantee that if the system disk was returned with the seal unbroken they would receive their money back. The manufacturer removed the risk of purchase with a simply administrated system. The cost of the sample floppy disk, which the customer kept, was easily outweighed by the interest earned on the early receipt of cash.

Packaging is also important when considering export markets. To achieve the necessary size and profits for a public flotation it is usually necessary for Australian companies to have an export strategy. Cultural differences can spring some nasty surprises. Asians consider reds and yellows as colours of quality while Anglo-Saxons consider them tawdry. Southern Europeans like serif type faces while Northern Europeans prefer Helvetica.

While some brands have created a global image, such as the Coke bottle and the McDonald's golden arches, other companies market differentiated products. In the US Campbell's soups have a famous red and white label, immortalised by the pop artist Andy Warhol, but in the United Kingdom Campbell's has positioned its products with a variety of labels.

Exports

As indicated above, a necessary requirement for building an Australian public company may be to develop an export strategy. One obvious target is the US with its population of 240 million and a Gross National Product about twenty times Australia's, similar language and customs, and plenty of market research supplied by US television and products. However, there are differences, particularly in the banking, legal, and industrial relations systems. The US is a fragmented market and should be regarded as 100 cities equivalent in size to Sydney or Melbourne. Each area requires a tailored approach, as the variations can be startling. Two marketing strategies are available: either buy a company or start up an office from scratch.

The first strategy, while probably the most cost-effective for most large companies, can be disastrous. A famous example is HC Sleigh, which paid $20 million for 50% of a US coal trading company, AOV. A few months later AOV went into receivership. The concern about the effect on HC Sleigh's profits depressed its share price and it was taken over. Private companies are difficult to audit and analyse. The fragmented banking system in the US makes credit analysis more difficult, compounding the problem. Thus the second alternative, of setting up your own office, is probably preferable for many small companies. The question then becomes whether you use an American or an Australian to head the operation. Again opinions vary but limited experience suggests it is better to use someone familiar with the company and the product to start up operations. There are of course excellent entrepreneurs and managers in the US. The problem is that they are almost impossible to recruit. It is more likely that the Australian company will end up with a second-rate operator. Television and tourism have helped us all feel far more comfortable dealing with overseas businesspeople. Indeed, while it would be a mistake to promote aggressively the Australian characteristics of the business it can certainly help to create corporate differentiation. Also, a visit to Australia by prospective customers can be a very effective sales weapon. The cost and time to enter the US should not be underestimated. A US office will require at least $500 000 in start-up funding and take at least twelve months to generate sales.

The other export markets which are becoming popular are the Asian markets. The cost of start-up here can be considerably lower than in the US. As a general rule, if the dominant language is English (such as in Singapore), you can set up a greenfields operation. On the other hand, for non-English-speaking cultures such as Thailand it is far safer to set up a joint venture with a local partner.

Promotion and advertising

For a new Australian consumer product a major problem is the concentration of buying power in the retail industry. The emergence of buying chains has made new product introduction more difficult. Typically, in the grocery trade new products are given only twelve weeks to prove themselves. Also, the retail chains have introduced a new-line fee to cover the introduction of new products. A common charge would be $250 000. In addition, at least $500 000 is probably required for the advertising launch. At least $750 000 and nearer to $1 million is probably the minimum marketing funding required to launch a new consumer product.

Hershey, a company with an excellent reputation, tried to launch its chocolate products in Australia and spent $500 000 on advertising. The competitive advertising budgets were estimated to be $6 million for Cadburys and $5 million for Mars and Rowntree Hoadley. The launch failed and retailers later said Hershey should have spent at least $3 million on advertising. These figures, combined with the knowledge that over 90 per cent of new consumer products wither and die within eighteen months, help explain why venture capitalists generally reject investment proposals based on consumer products.

On the other hand, consumer products that have a self-financing form of distribution are attractive. Direct mail is one approach, franchising is another. Franchising has been a popular form of investment in the US, representing about 10 per cent of venture capital. The size of the market in the US means sufficient branches can be established so only a small royalty is required to cover central-office overheads. In Australia the market is smaller so creating an adequately sized network is more difficult. The product must have sufficient gross margin to provide satisfactory profits for both the franchiser and franchisee. Only a few products, such as pizza and tax planning, have sufficient gross margins. Otherwise, franchisers must obtain their returns from either supply of the product (Mr Whippy) or asset growth by leasing the premises (McDonald's). The high risk and entry cost of consumer products result in most venture capitalists preferring industrial products, which can also be sold to government entities when they have established credibility in the marketplace.

The product life cycle

It is important to recognise that every market contains potential purchasers as well as actual ones and at the time a new product or service is launched practically the whole of the market represents 'potential'. Converting potential purchasers into actual ones takes time; it will often take between five and twenty years before 90 per cent of the members of a particular group have adopted a new product.

Within an established market, a new product will take a similar length of time to become generally recognised as a practical and efficient alternative to the established products. Over such a long period the market itself changes: some people die, or become too old to participate in the market, or migrate away from the market. At the same time, immigration and children growing up will increase the market size. Some people may become too poor to buy the products, while others may reach a sufficient level of affluence to enter the market.

A decision to enter a market for the first time, or to change to a new product, will often be sufficiently significant as to require considerable investigation and management resources. Inexperienced start-up entrepreneurs are hurt and bewildered to learn that their potential customers continue to buy old and inferior products. If they study those customers closely, they will find that they are ordinary people with many other demands on their time. Investigating a new product or service may be fairly low on their priority list.

For most markets that have been studied, no more than 5 per cent, and often less than 1 per cent, of the potential purchasers targeted by advertising, point of sale and other promotional material, and sales 'cold calls' actually enter a new market or buy a new product in the year following the product's launch.

Most people do not have time to make a careful personal investigation of a new market or a new product, and do so vicariously. When a trusted friend or colleague has used a new product, and praises it, people who have not *personally* examined it in detail will become significantly more likely to buy it for themselves or their business. This 'internal growth' among users of a new product can amount to between 25 per cent and 75 per cent of the growth in demand for a new product. It tapers off as the number of actual users rises and the number of potential ones falls. The combined effect of a few of the potential users responding to the marketing effort while many more respond to the influence of those who have already joined the market gives the product life cycle its characteristic shape (Figure 12.3).

These facts must be taken into account when estimating sales in future years, and particularly when estimating the time it will take for a new venture to break even. Under some circumstances, a venture must be replanned at this point—if not cancelled. If, for example, a new product is unlikely to get more than 15 per cent market share, and needs a market share of 12 per cent to break even, it probably never will.

Figure 12.3 shows a product (or market) life cycle for a fairly attractive product (such as a VCR). Note that although 97 per cent of potential purchasers will be using the product fifteen

Figure 12.3 The product life cycle

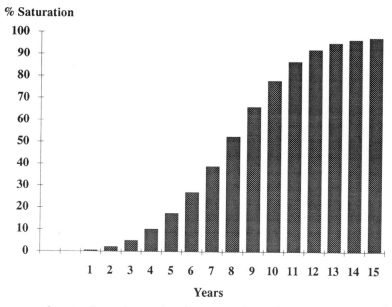

years after its launch, in the first year less than 1 per cent of potential users adopt the product and enter the market. The model used to produce Figure 12.3 is very basic; more sophisticated models take into account factors like the entry of competitors and life cycle price changes. The effort required to develop a life cycle model is usually amply repaid.

13 Preparing a business plan: the financial analysis

In this chapter we examine the techniques of financial analysis which demonstrate to potential investors that the entrepreneur understands the business.

When they describe their business finances, many company annual reports and many businesspeople do so with a pie chart, similar to Figure 13.1. The chart demonstrates how much of every sales dollar the company must pay for labour and materials, interest payments and taxes. Usually the chairperson's report contains some comment about how little is left for dividends and retained earnings.

Unfortunately the diagram is misleading. It implies that in every dollar of sales there is an element of profit. The pie chart illustrates the misconception that the basic equation of business is the same as the profit and loss statement: sales–costs = profit.

Breakeven analysis uses a different and more realistic approach. Every business has two types of costs. Fixed costs are those costs that must be paid irrespective of sales. Examples are rent, utilities, management salaries and so on. No profit can be earned unless the fixed costs are covered. Variable costs refer to those costs that vary according to sales. Examples are raw materials, manufacturing labour costs, transport and warranty provisions. The actual business equation is as follows:

Sales–Variable costs = Contribution

Contribution–Fixed costs = Profit

The equation is often portrayed in chart form as shown in Figure 13.2. As the sales increase so the profit increases, as indicated by the rising profit line. The angle of the profit line depends on the contribution. The greater the contribution per dollar of sales the steeper the gradient of the profit line. If sales are zero, the loss is equal to the fixed costs or where the profit line cuts the Y-axis. If there are sufficient sales that the contribution equals the fixed costs, the business is at breakeven (the

Figure 13.1 Typical division of sales dollar

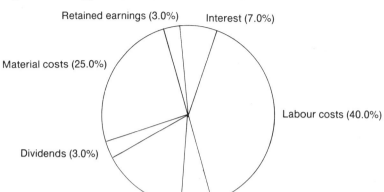

profit is zero) and the breakeven point is where the profit line cuts the X-axis.

The first step in breakeven analysis is to calculate the contribution rate. This is usually expressed as a percentage and defined as follows:

$$\frac{(Sales - Variable\,costs)}{Sales} = Contribution\ rate$$

The gross margin (sales less cost of goods sold) is often taken as a surrogate for contribution. The approximation assumes identical stock levels at the beginning and end of the accounting year.

The breakeven point is then calculated by dividing the fixed costs by the contribution rate. The breakeven point may be expressed as a sales figure ('We need $30 000 sales a month to break even'). If the business is dominated by a single product or has a standard measure of volume, the breakeven point can be expressed in physical terms ('We need to carry 5000 passengers a day').

A simple business may sell $50 000 worth of product a month, have a cost of goods sold of $30 000 and show a profit before tax of $4000. What is its breakeven point?

Sales	$50 000
Variable costs	− $30 000
Contribution	= $20 000
Fixed costs	− $16 000

Figure 13.2 Typical breakeven chart

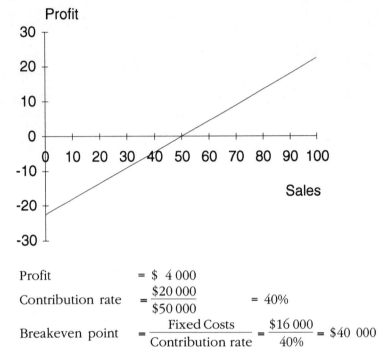

Profit	= $ 4 000
Contribution rate	$= \dfrac{\$20\,000}{\$50\,000} = 40\%$
Breakeven point	$= \dfrac{\text{Fixed Costs}}{\text{Contribution rate}} = \dfrac{\$16\,000}{40\%} = \$40\,000$

Breakeven analysis can be used to predict profits. What would be the profitability at $60 000 sales per month? This is solved by using the equation:

Profit = (Sales – Breakeven point) × Contribution rate
= (60 000 – 40 000) × 40%
= $8 000

Increasing sales by 20 per cent doubles the profits of the business. Breakeven analysis is a fundamental tool of successful entrepreneurs. They should calculate it every accounting period. Every business has a different breakeven chart. As shown in Figures 13.3 and 13.4, manufacturing companies typically have high fixed costs and high contribution rates while retail organisations have low fixed costs and low contribution rates.

Besides providing a tool for predicting profits at different levels of sales and understanding the dynamics of a business, breakeven analysis can be useful when deciding on business strategy. Profits can be increased by increasing sales volume,

Figure 13.3 Manufacturing company breakeven chart

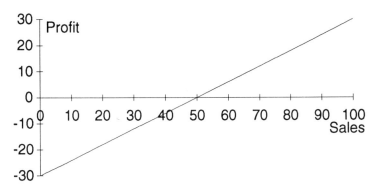

reducing fixed costs or increasing the contribution rate. If each variable can be altered by 10 per cent with equivalent effort, then the calculations for one business would be as shown in Table 13.1. Readers should repeat the four calculations themselves to ensure they understand breakeven points. In this simple example, the strategy of either increasing sales (by a new advertising campaign, say) or increasing the contribution rate (by changing transport companies, for example) would be equally profitable.

While the example above is simple, calculating the effect of cost reductions on the breakeven point is usually illuminating.

The contribution rate can be increased in three ways:

- increasing selling prices, which is probably the most common technique;
- changing the product mix to increase the total contribution

Table 13.1 Breakeven variations

	Base case	10% increase in sales	10% decrease in fixed costs	10% increase in contribution
Sales	$50 000	$55 000	$50 000	$50 000
Variable costs	$30 000	$33 000	$30 000	$28 000
Contribution	$20 000	$22 000	$20 000	$22 000
Fixed costs	$16 000	$16 000	$14 000	$16 000
Profit before tax	$ 4 000	$ 6 000	$ 5 600	$ 6 000
Contribution rate	40%	40%	40%	44%
Breakeven point	$40 000	$40 000	$36 000	$36 364

Figure 13.4   Retail company breakeven chart

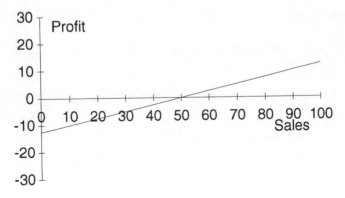

rate by replacing low margin products with higher margin products; and

- decreasing variable costs by switching suppliers or introducing labour-saving equipment.

Breakeven analysis is also useful for providing a format for cash flow forecasts. In every business plan there must be a section on financial projections. A business plan without projections is like a body without a heart. The quality of the financial projections is of key importance to venture capital investors. The task for entrepreneurs is to prepare a valid set of projections. Presentation is also of paramount importance.

Financial projections have three components:

- monthly cash flows;
- annual profit and loss statements; and
- annual balance sheets.

The monthly cash flows should extend for at least twelve months after the cash flow turnaround. It helps to plot a cumulative cash flow curve, as shown in Figure 13.5. The cash flow curve is similar to the economists' 'J' curve for the balance of payments following a devaluation. Capital expenditure, set-up costs and working capital burn up cash, then as sales occur the cash flow turns from negative to positive.

When laying out the cash flows, label the months as month 1, month 2, starting from the first capital injection. Otherwise you will need to constantly update the projections during the negotiations.

Figure 13.5 Cumulative cash flow curve

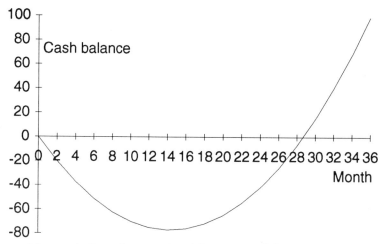

The cash flow layout should consist of four sections:

- operating cash in (sales, royalties, etc.);
- operating cash out (material, labour, rents, etc.);
- capital expenditure; and
- financing cash flows (debt, equity, interest, and dividends).

Operating cash in refers to cash received. Cash received comes from sales or government grants and not from financing. The key is to first make a sales estimate and then, using a lag of two to three months, estimate the debtors. Most entrepreneurs underestimate the debtors requirements. It is worth noting the actual figures in sales-days for some groups of listed companies. Average debtors typically vary between 40 and 60 sales-days (see Table 13.2).

Operating cash out is calculated in several steps. Step one is to work out the labour and material requirements for the variable cost section of the operating costs. This will vary from business to business. However it is worth noting stock levels and creditors for certain businesses. Typical ratios are 60 sales-days of stock held and 35 sales-days for creditors. Step two is to work out the cash flows of the fixed costs such as management, sales administration, research and development.

The third group of cash flows are the capital expenditures. Tax payments should also be calculated. Taxable income will

Table 13.2　Working capital ratios in sales-days for listed companies

Group	Stock	Debtors	Creditors
Builders suppliers	55	51	36
Chemicals	88	56	28
Food manufacturing	56	38	37
Paper and packaging	70	52	28
Retail	49	4	22
Textiles	107	62	29

be equal to net operating cash flow less depreciation and provisions. Tax is typically paid nine months in arrears but recently has varied from Budget to Budget.

After calculating the operating cash flows the next step is to prepare the financing cash flows. The usual technique is to first calculate the cash flows as if the financing were 100 per cent equity and no dividends. Then introduce debt financing into the model. It is necessary to do an iterative calculation, for interest will reduce the taxable income and in turn reduce the rate of repayment of debt.

After completing the cash flows the entrepreneur needs to prepare profit and loss accounts and balance sheets. The preferred layouts below are described in full in Appendix A.

One format for the pro-forma Profit & Loss Statement is:

Sales
- Cost of goods sold
= Gross profit
- Selling, general & administration
= Earnings before interest and taxation
- Interest
= Pre-tax profit
- Tax
= Post-tax profit

One format for the pro-forma Balance Sheet is:

Current assets
+ Fixed assets
+ Intangible assets
= Total assets

Current liabilities

+ Long term liabilities

+ Shareholders' funds or equity

Total liabilities and equity

Then a number of ratios should be calculated. The key ratios are:

Net margin

This percentage is calculated by dividing the post-tax profits by the sales. Anything over 10 per cent is suspicious.

Gearing

This is expressed as the percentage total debt represents of shareholders' funds and is a measure of financial risk. Anything over 100 per cent is regarded as high.

Stock, creditors, and debtors ratios

These are collectively known as the working capital ratios. They should be calculated in terms of sales-days or annual sales divided by 365. Anything below 60 sales-days of stock, below 50 sales-days of debtors or above 40 sales-days of creditors is probably unrealistic.

Return on equity

The return on equity equals post-tax profits divided by shareholders' funds expressed as a percentage. The return on equity should be above 15 per cent.

Interest cover

This ratio is defined as pre-interest cash flow divided by interest payments. If the interest cover falls below 2, the financing risk of the business is too high.

Annual sales/employee

This ratio should be calculated monthly but expressed as an annual figure. To calculate it you need to prepare a workforce planning chart which shows the monthly growth in staff. The monthly sales figures from your cash flow forecasts are then matched with the monthly workforce totals. Publicly listed companies vary from a low of $80 000 to a high of $200 000. If your figures fall outside this range your workforce estimates are probably too low or your sales growth estimates are too high.

Contribution and breakeven point

These two ratios should also be calculated on a monthly basis for the business. As a check you should also include detailed manufacturing cost calculations for the two or three most popular products.

As indicated previously, such calculations would have been very time-consuming and expensive before the introduction of personal computers. With the advent of spread-sheets, they are now easy to prepare and should take two to three days at most. Moreover, if your financial estimates are available on a spreadsheet you can change or modify your estimates relatively effortlessly.

One mistake entrepreneurs make is to project at a detailed level too far into the future. Remember the plan should fit into a briefcase. Including pages of spreadsheets will try the patience of most investors. One page for annual profit and loss statements, balance sheets, and ratios combined with two to three pages for cash flows and workforce estimates is often enough. The back-up documentation should be available but not included. On the other hand, key assumptions in the estimates should also be stated in the financial section.

Samuel Goldwyn once said it is difficult to prophesy, especially about the future. If there is a consensus about forecasts it is that to try and make them for a ten-year period is impossible—just budgeting for eighteen months ahead is difficult enough. Entrepreneurs should have their minds fixed on two key dates. How long will it take before the business turns cash-flow-positive, and in what year will net profit after tax exceed $1 million? The financial analysis should provide a good indication of those two dates.

14 Preparing a business plan: organisational and operational issues

The operational and organisational issues of importance to investors comprise the final significant part of a business plan. Among these are the organisational structure, quality of management, implementation plan, environmental threats, protection of intellectual property and employee ownership of shares.

The first key task is to have a management team organised. The ideal management team should include people with skills in selling, finance and administration, operations and product development. Typically some necessary skills are missing but usually a start-up needs at least three individuals. There should be someone who understands and can sell to the market, there should be someone who can develop and manufacture the product, and someone who can handle finance and administration.

As important as having key individuals on board is ensuring relatives and friends are not freeloading off the company. Both the management and board of the company should comprise competent people who are interested in increasing the net worth of the business.

The best indication of quality of management is a track record in the industry. A good example of this would be the Sock Shop, a UK retail chain that specialises in hosiery. In the first four years of operation the company set up 59 small shops. In the fourth year turnover and net profits were $35 million and $3 million respectively. The company floated after three years when net profit exceeded $1 million. The management team is a husband and wife. The wife began her career in the typing pool of Marks and Spencer, the largest retailer in the UK, and worked her way up to become the chairman's secretary. She left to help start the Tie Rack, a chain of speciality tie shops, where she met her husband, a chartered accountant. In the 18 months they both worked at the Tie Rack, the number of stores went from zero to fifteen. This team of two together had the three key skills of sales, operations and accounting and also a track record in the industry. Many investors rejected their business plan. After four years the company had a market valuation of over $125 million.

The business plan must include an implementation plan. This should start with a statement of the two or three key objectives the company will accomplish in each of the next two to three years. The plan should then contain a reasonably detailed operational checklist of the various steps that are going to happen in each calendar quarter. If these objectives are displayed in chart form showing the start date and duration of each activity, so much the better.

After the operational plan there should be a section on external obstacles to success. These may be legal restrictions and regulations or problems with unions. Other difficulties may result from the manufacturing process. Aquaculture businesses, for example, must consider problems of food supply, temperature, energy costs, disease and predators.

The operation section should address the ownership of intellectual property. Intellectual property refers to those intangible assets of a company which are a result of invention or creative thinking. Many federal laws cover the protection of intellectual property. Among the more important are the patents, copyright, design, trademarks and trade practices acts.

Patents are the best-known form of intellectual property protection. Patent applications are valid if the invention is new, not in the public domain, and applies to a new substance, machine or process. Patents are expensive to obtain and cost $2000–$3000 per country. A worldwide patent could cost more than $300 000. Thus inventors may choose only to patent their invention in certain countries. To keep a patent the holder may have to prove the invention has not been in the public domain. Otherwise the patent will not hold. There have been some unfortunate examples, such as the invention of monoclonal antibodies, where the desire of the academic to publish meant that patent protection was refused. Another problem with patents is that although governments grant patents they do not enforce them. Enforcement rests with the patent holder, who must go to court to stop infringements. It is the court that enforces patents. Another drawback with patents is the time taken to process the patent application.

The first step in getting a patent is to lodge a provisional specification, which is a brief description of the invention. The date of lodgement of the provisional specification is known as the 'priority date', which a court will use to establish claims. Within twelve months the applicant must lodge a complete specification with descriptions and drawings, otherwise the provisional application will lapse. Once the complete specification is lodged, and up to a maximum of eighteen months after the priority date, the patent office publishes the complete specifications to allow the public to inspect and to object. Within five years of lodging the complete specification you must request examination by the Australian Patent Office, which, if satisfied the invention is 'new', will grant the patent. The patent stays in force provided the annual fee is paid for sixteen years from the date of lodgement of the complete specification.

Another problem is that for some products, such as medical ones, sixteen years is insufficient time to complete testing, launch the product, and recover costs. Indeed a major industry has developed in the US for the generic production of those popular drugs whose patents have run out. To speed up the patent process there is a lower order of patents, called petty patents, which allow the inventor to patent just one part of an invention. Petty patents last initially for one year and may be extended for a further five. A common strategy is now to go for a petty patent and extend it to a full patent if the product becomes a commercial success.

Another problem with patents, especially with the advent of electronic databases, is that on publication the invention is in the public domain. Hence many companies now avoid patents and rely on other techniques of protection. While a patent is no guarantee of uniqueness, it is wise for entrepreneurs to carry out a patent search. A patent attorney or entrepreneurs themselves can do this at the patent office. It is not difficult and the patent office can be very helpful.

The advantage of the patent process is that it can be used as a negotiating tool if the entrepreneur or inventor decides the more profitable course of action is to license the technology. The inventor first lodges a provisional patent and, in the twelve months before lodging a complete specification, negotiates with several licensees. As a potential bargaining weapon the inventor can threaten to put the invention in the public domain so nobody has unique licensing rights.

Because of the sixteen-year time span for patents, intellec-

tual property is better protected by copyright. Copyright protects
the material form but not the idea itself. Computer programs,
company manuals and silicon chip designs are examples of
items that may now be subject to protection by copyright.
Copyright rests with the author of a work except if he is an
employee; in which case it rests with the employer. Protection
typically lasts for 50 years after the death of the author. Copyright prevents copying of the original material form, such as an
instruction manual, whereas patents provide a total monopoly
which stops either production or use of an invention or process.
However, as copyright protection arises when the work is produced and costs almost nothing, copyright protection is often
sought because there is no delay as with patents.

Designs and trademarks are not regarded as vital for high
growth business. They are for buy-outs, where often a trade-
mark (which can last forever) may be a key asset of the
company.

Because patent registration means publication, more and
more companies are using the protection provided by trade
secrets. Many companies ask both their customers, employees
and suppliers to sign confidentiality agreements, either explicitly
or as a term in a supply contract. In any trade secrets action
part of the onus of proof is on the prosecutors, who must
demonstrate that they have made reasonable efforts to keep the
product or method secret.

The courts, after years of siding with defenders, are now
beginning to side with the prosecutors over patent, trade
secrets, and copyright infringements. For example, Kodak had
to close down its instant camera division following a successful
action by Polaroid.

While some investors may be excited by patents, most prefer
intellectual property to be protected by secrecy arrangements.
What granted patents do provide to the investor is a limited
proof of uniqueness.

In the area of employment compensation, the business plan
should cover two topics: the company's policies on Employee
Stock Ownership Plans (ESOPs) and employment contracts.
ESOPs are part of the venture capital game in the US. It is almost
an article of faith that employees should be able to acquire
shares at a low cost and, if the company becomes successful
and lists, share in the fruits. For example, in the week following
the initial public offering of Apollo Computers, 39 new Merce-

des appeared in the employees' parking lot! In the US special tax concessions exist which treat favourably employees who have received shares as an incentive.

In Australia the position is unfortunately different, with a more complicated tax structure. Furthermore, the US experience indicates share distribution should be limited. If employees holding shares later leave the company, they may cause difficulties and be an impediment to the company's growth.

A common technique to avoid undue share dispersion prior to listing is to interpose a company or a unit trust called an Employee Share Ownership Trust (ESOT). The board or trustee will typically be a new company with the same board of directors as the issuing company. Employees are invited to take up issues of units depending on seniority and length of service.

The next problem is to eliminate the tax burden created by section 26AAC of the Income Tax Act. Effectively, an employee shareholder who buys a share at a discount to market value will pay tax on the discount. Since July 1988 a discount of 10 per cent of the market price is now tax free provided the total amount of the discount is less than $200. If the share is subject to conditions or restrictions of sale or if title to the share may be rendered null and void (if, for example, the employee leaves the company), tax is assessable when the restrictions are removed or the share is sold.

One structure is to create a special class of partly paid shares which are paid to 1c. These shares are entitled to dividends and capital profits but only participate on liquidation to the amount of capital paid. Another technique is to issue options on shares. If the employee believes the value of the shares is going to rise he or she may elect under 28AAC to be assessed in the year the option was acquired on the value of the share less the exercise price less the issue cost of the option. Any capital profit the employee makes will still be assessable under the capital gains legislation, but both the option cost and purchase price will be indexed from the time of elected assessment. Options may be granted for up to five years and typically are non-exercisable if the employee leaves the company.

People usually underestimate the benefits of indexation due to inflation. In the US the capital gains tax rate is 28 per cent compared to 39 per cent in Australia. For an inflation rate of 7 per cent, the Australian rate is less after a holding period of five years.

While capital gains tax is a negative, dividend imputation is
a most positive measure for designing effective staff incentive
schemes. By having partly paid shares that are entitled to full
dividends and dividends which are fully franked, employees can
pay the remainder due on their shares with a tax-free income
stream. The company will also retain the capital for further
growth. Moreover, employees can be given an interest free loan
to purchase employee shares, which is one of the few benefits
not subject to fringe benefits tax.

Another way of using dividend imputation is to pay dividends to employees instead of bonuses. As an example, compare an employee earning $19,500 a year who is paid a 15 per
cent salary bonus to an employee on the same salary paid a
7.65 per cent bonus as dividend. The figure of 7.65 per cent
assumes the company is paying tax at the full rate of 39 per
cent.

Bonus paid as salary	
Annual salary	$19 500
Tax paid	5 639
Take-home pay	13 861
15% bonus paid as salary	
Extra payment	2 925
Tax paid (40% marginal rate)	1 170
Post-tax income	1 755
Final take-home pay	$15 616
	(a 12.7% increase)
Bonus paid as dividend	
Extra Payment	$1 492
Grossed-up income	2 925
Add to current wage	19 500
Total income	22 425
Tax payable	6 809
Less tax credit	(1 433)
Tax payable	5 375
After-tax income	$17 049
	(a 23% increase)

Indeed, paying a dividend out of post-tax income has two
additional benefits. The company establishes itself as a divi-
dend-paying stock. And it has a minimal effect on the invest-

ment analysts, who tend to look at annual profits after tax rather than retained earnings.

The second topic in the employment compensation area is employment contracts. Experience demonstrates that such contracts favour the employee far more than the employer. If entrepreneurs need the security of a contract and are insufficiently confident of their job, can investors be confident about the business? Equity should be a sufficient tie and adequate reward. The company policy set at board level should be not to have employment contracts.

15 Choosing a venture capitalist

Once a company has been formed, a business plan prepared and one or two successful businesspeople attracted as board members, a platform on which to raise money has been established.

The next step is to contact venture capitalists and organise a presentation. Entrepreneurs should remember they are on a selling exercise—what they are selling is part of the company. For consideration they are obtaining cash plus intangible costs and benefits.

The money invested will usually be coloured by the investor's reputation. Investors with good reputations are invaluable. As mentioned earlier, part of the venture capital game is the continual round of money-raising. Entrepreneurs should expect support from early investors in raising extra funds. Important in the fund-raising is the reputation of early investors. Entrepreneurs must establish the character of the investment company. If it is listed, you can ask a stock broker. Another method is find out who is on the board of the venture capital company and examine their credentials.

The easiest way to find out who the directors of the venture capital company are is to ask for the annual report. Annual reports are most useful documents. Besides stating who the directors are, they can provide other information. First, entrepreneurs should be able to establish how much of the funds is invested and how much is available for new investments. Venture capitalists typically invest around 75 per cent of funds under management and aim at keeping 25 per cent in reserve. The annual report is also probably out of date, so entrepreneurs should ask such questions as, 'In your latest annual report I noted you had invested $5 million out of a possible $11 million; is that ratio still valid or have there been any changes?'

Annual reports of venture capital companies, besides providing an indication of the funds available, usually also contain a summary of individual investments. From reading it, entrepreneurs should be able to develop a feel for the type and size of investments. If the average investment is $100 000 and you are seeking $1 million, then you may have a problem.

Annual reports also provide the names of referees. Entrepreneurs can contact the managing directors of the investments and find out what the venture capitalists are like as investors and partners. Venture capitalists, if they become interested in a proposition, should spend a lot of time checking the entrepreneur's references. There is no reason why entrepreneurs should not act similarly.

The annual report will also provide the names of the company's auditors and lawyers. While entrepreneurs can also use them as referees, they must be more circumspect. On the other hand, auditors and lawyers or investment managing directors can be used as introducers. Entrepreneurs who ask them for an introduction and reinforce the request with a business plan and creditable board members may well get an associate of the venture capitalist to carry out an introduction. Even better, the introducer may persuade the venture capitalist to ring the entrepreneur. Either method is preferable to either sending in the business plan unsolicited or leaving it behind after a cold-call presentation.

Another key criterion is distance. The farther the business is from the money the smaller the probability of gaining funds. The more successful American venture capitalists, when they are expected to be the lead investor, refuse to consider any business where the head office is located at more than 90 minutes travelling distance. Venture capital requires hands-on involvement and being too far away can be a knockout. Entrepreneurs are encouraged to adopt a focused approach to venture capital. The Australian venture capitalist community is so small that a project being offered to all investors is soon dismissed. A similar environment existed in Silicon Valley during the 1970s when the venture capital community was small and self-contained.

Another important factor is the stage of the investment. Early-stage investors include MICs, private individuals and public sector financial institutions. Most private institutional venture capital financiers tend to concentrate on second stage financing.

Most venture capitalists regard themselves as hands-on investors, and the most common form of interaction will be at board level. Entrepreneurs should find out early who is going to sit on the board, what is their experience in business, and what has been the experience of other entrepreneurs with them as directors. Entrepreneurs should also establish how often they will have contact with the venture capitalists. Ideally venture capitalists should talk to the entrepreneur at least once a week and visit say once a fortnight. If a venture capitalist is sitting on the boards of twelve companies and nominates someone else to maintain contact, it is a warning to the entrepreneur that there will be little contact with him.

The first visit will probably be by the entrepreneur to the office of the venture capitalist. If the venture capitalist prefers to visit the entrepreneur first, that can be taken as an encouraging sign about the calibre of the venture capitalist. The entrepreneur should have a short (fifteen minute) presentation on the company prepared, covering the mission statement, staff, the market, competition and financial requirements. Many ventures are now using videos, but in my opinion, videos turn off an experienced investor just like business plans prepared by accountants. The first meeting is principally about establishing credibility for both parties. Further meetings will get down to negotiation of the deal, and that is the subject of the next chapter.

16 Negotiations with venture capitalists

Negotiation is often compared to a game of poker. At first glance the odds would appear to heavily favour the venture capitalist. The venture capitalist has the money. The venture capitalist can walk away from the game and still have the money. The venture capitalist is repeatedly dealing with entrepreneurs, so his or her negotiating skills are continually being honed, while the entrepreneur seldom meets with investors.

On the other hand, entrepreneurs should remember that while a venture capitalist may see many deals, few merit investment. If your proposal attracts the venture capitalist, then you have crossed the first hurdle. Furthermore, entrepreneurs can use the same weapon monopoly sellers have always used—the threat of a counter offer. If the venture capitalist is aware that you are discussing your proposal with other investors it can well speed up and help complete the negotiations.

It is useful to note the characteristics of good (defined as tough) negotiators. Good negotiators typically:

- open with a very high but realistic demand;
- make a few small concessions but no large ones;
- decrease their concessions as negotiations continue; and
- are undisturbed by threats of deadlock but are conscious of methods of avoiding deadlock.

In venture capital negotiations the first key variable is the pre-funding valuation placed on the company before injecting funds. Valuations are discussed more thoroughly in Chapter 18 but the key equation, assuming all money invested stays within the company (the investors will subscribe to newly issued shares), is:

$$\text{Pre--funding valuation} = \frac{\text{funds invested}}{\% \text{ of company owned}} - \text{funds invested}$$

For example, a company with an issued capital of 3 million shares issues a further 1 million shares for $500 000. Then:

$$\text{Pre-funding valuation} = \frac{(\$500\,000)}{25\%} - \$500\,000$$

$$= \$1.5\,\text{million}$$

It is important for entrepreneurs to realise there is no one true valuation of a private company.

The valuations of public companies can vary substantially, as any reader of the financial pages who has followed takeovers would be aware. For private companies the range can be even greater. However, while the range may be wide it is not infinite. Entrepreneurs should aim at the high end of the realistic range. Moreover, there are many other negotiating issues besides valuation. While the business plan (which may be considered as the opening offer) may omit these topics, they will be negotiating points.

Whatever structure the business plan proposes will almost certainly be modified. Venture capitalists seek several financial objectives in a deal. These objectives are generally met by the structure of a deal. Structure refers to the number and type of shares issued and the mix of equity, debt, options and guarantees given.

Every business plan contains financial projections—venture capitalists know from bitter experience that the likelihood of entrepreneurs meeting projections is low. In the expectation that the company will fail to meet the forecasts, venture capitalists often suggest that they take a bigger share of the company at the start but have options granted to entrepreneurs related to performance. To counter this proposal entrepreneurs may suggest that options over part of the entrepreneurs' shares be granted to the venture capitalists if the performance is poorer than projected.

Another concern of the venture capitalist is that although the company may grow and prosper, entrepreneurs may change their objectives and decide to stay as head of a private company. If this change of plan occurs, the venture capitalists will have capital tied up in the company with no opportunity of recovery. Consequently, venture capitalists often seek to invest in the form of redeemable preference shares so they have the opportunity to redeem their original investment. Other venture capitalists choose a hybrid debt/equity instrument where the debt may be converted to equity if the company goes public. Examples of these so called 'Irish equity' instruments are convertible notes or a subordinated loan with options. Entrepreneurs should seek to bank the investment as equity. While they will be continually seeking rounds of equity, they may need to use debt as bridging finance between rounds. A key ratio for lending institutions is the debt/equity ratio. The enterprise will find it difficult to borrow if there is already excessive debt on the balance sheet.

Once the valuation and structure are agreed, entrepreneurs should obtain a letter of intent or term sheet. This is a two- to three-page document that contains the amount and type of investment, a list of the representations and warranties required, and the affirmative and negative covenants.

The representations and warranties are defined in the shareholders' agreement. Typical requirements are evidence of incorporation, schedules of leases and assets, latest audited accounts, schedules of insurance, and so on. On behalf of the company, entrepreneurs will then disclose the state of the company; the disclosures are attached as appendices to the agreement. These documents take some time to prepare and asking for what is required earlier rather than later lends a sense of urgency to the negotiations.

The affirmative covenants are a list of actions entrepreneurs agree to carry out as long as the venture capitalist is an investor in the company. Common requirements are monthly board meetings, regular financial statements, payment of all government taxes, regular filings and maintenance of company records, preparation of an annual budget, and so on.

The negative covenants are a list of actions entrepreneurs will not allow to occur without the approval of the investors. Common terms are increases in salary of key executives, purchase or lease of capital equipment above certain limits, acquisition or merger with another company, and changes in capital structure. These three areas of warranties, affirmative covenants and negative covenants should all be regarded as negotiable. Entrepreneurs should not be averse to asking why a clause is included. They will gain credibility with investors if their objections are thoughtful and sensible.

Board composition is often a contentious topic. It is well worth spending some time on it, because it will play an important role in developing the company. Entrepreneurs should aim at having a right of veto of appointment. A growing business typically goes from crisis to crisis. These crises tend to erupt at board meetings, and having inexperienced external directors who understand neither the technology nor the market can be disastrous.

A final negotiating point is the payment of legal fees. This is a common procedure in the US and is also attempted in Australia. In fact a company in Australia is unable to pay for the legal fees owing to the Corporations Law, which prohibits companies from purchasing or aiding in the purchase of their shares except in special cases. Venture capitalists may ask entrepreneurs to pay the legal fees or make some other form of payment as advisory fees. As a minimum, entrepreneurs should put a cap on the fees paid. Somehow discussions tend to be shorter if both parties are paying the bills instead of just one.

On completion of the term sheet negotiations, the lawyers will draft and negotiate the shareholders' agreement. If the venture capitalist has any 'form', a standard document should be available. Here entrepreneurs have to accept the golden rule of business: 'He who has the gold makes the rules.' On the other hand, you should have your legal officer inspect the document and list in order of priority the key clauses to negotiate and those susceptible to concession. Lawyers tend to treat all points of issue as material while the commercial reality is that perhaps only 20 per cent are of commercial importance. One common technique of negotiation is to adopt a tough stance on all points and, if you think it necessary to concede, to do so on a point of minor importance.

The shareholders' agreement should follow the outline of the term sheet. You should as an intelligent entrepreneur have accounts audited by a big accounting firm. Investors asking for a further audit should be told that will be fine as long as they pay for it.

A key part of the shareholders' agreement is the warranties. The investor will ask entrepreneurs to make a series of statements about the company, such as that no government taxes and duties are outstanding, the bad debt provisions are adequate, there are no lawsuits against the company and so on. Investors rely on the word of entrepreneurs, and the shareholders' agreement is the formal crystallisation of this. Many entrepreneurs become unduly concerned by the warranties. First, they should remember that once they have made the disclosure and venture capitalists subsequently invest, then the venture capitalists will have no recourse. Disclosure actually protects entrepreneurs more than venture capitalists and the policy should be to disclose everything. The tactic entrepreneurs should adopt is to try to ensure that included in each of the warranties is a disclaimer, along the lines: 'The entrepreneur has taken such fair and reasonable action as a businessperson would take to ensure, etc.' Entrepreneurs should then take fair and reasonable action. With bad debts, for example, instead of just warranting that the provisions are adequate, it is better to warrant that for the past three years bad debts were $X representing Y per cent of debtors, and as of 'a date' the debtors' list showed the following debtors as more than 90 days due. Furthermore, on telephone contact all the 90-day debtors indicated payment would be made in 30 days. Entrepreneurs should get hold of the list of required warranties early and start acting on them as soon as realistically possible. While the list of required warranties is gradually becoming standard there are still significant differences among investors.

By now you may be wondering if the activity outlined in this section is worthwhile. Entrepreneurs should expect to spend at least six months, and up to a year, on preparing a business plan, meeting with venture capitalists, answering the due diligence questions and negotiating a shareholders' agreement. The time initially taken and then repeated annually is what makes the financial controller, who should be a qualified accountant, an important member of the initial entrepreneurial team. Most business textbooks stress the need for such an individual, particularly when the company employs more than a dozen people. A typical rationale is the need for a business to have accurate reporting and cash forecasting systems. While such requirements are mandatory, the main reason for employing a financial controller for a high-growth company is the need to have one person focused on raising the next round of finance.

Entrepreneurs should remember how to generate net worth. Net worth or shareholders' funds is defined as assets less liabilities. One objective of business is to increase the net worth of the company. Indeed, many successful entrepreneurs have used a steady annual increase in net worth as their fundamental business objective. The failure of many businesses to remember this objective is a common reason for their business difficulties.

One way to increase net worth is to increase assets. A typical technique of many high-tech companies is to capitalise research and development instead of writing it off against profit. Another common technique is to create some intangible asset such as intellectual property. Most people in the financial community are aware of such techniques of balance sheet improvement and will automatically remove such intangibles from the list of assets.

Another technique is to reduce liabilities; for most businesses this is done by leasing. Leasing can be effective, but entrepreneurs should remember that wide variations can occur in the marketplace. Annualised interest rates can vary by as much as 7 per cent over a four-year period. Such a difference could represent a total extra interest payment of over 30 per cent. Leasing is expensive and it pays to shop.

Thus, to increase shareholders' funds entrepreneurs have to produce retained earnings and raise new rounds of equity. They should compare the two methods. A good business operates on a post-tax margin of 5 per cent. To add $500 000 to shareholders' funds will therefore require $10 000 000 in sales. Ask most entrepreneurs if they would prepare a 30-page proposal, go through say twenty meetings, and negotiate a 30-page agreement for a $10 million contract, and the answers would be 'How? who? and when?' Ask the same entrepreneurs to prepare a 30-page business plan and negotiate with financiers and many will say it is too difficult. Successful entrepreneurs know raising equity is the easier task. What is required is the ability to learn and speak the language of the financier.

Another method of raising funds is to hire an investment banker or financial adviser. Many companies offer their services; few are satisfactory. Advisers can help in preparing a memorandum and may establish a realistic valuation. They can usually generate the first meeting with investors through their range of contacts. This can be useful if you are trying to attract institutional money. Financial advisers are useful during negotiations. They can be more aggressive negotiators and any stigma or bitterness should stay attached to them.

All sorts of companies are now involved in financial advisory work, ranging from accountants to the retail banks. Entrepreneurs should decide upon their advisers using the same criteria for choosing any service organisation: reputation, people, and price.

Contacts are important, especially when raising finance. Fund-raising is selling. When choosing a financial adviser, ask him or her to sell to you. Ask the adviser for three recent references and details of three recent deals. Finally, get some feeling for price. Typically fees are either on an hourly basis (accountants) or on a fee for success basis. Entrepreneurs should at least get an estimate for the job and ask for a 'cap'. With a fee for success the adviser takes a fee if the fund-raising is successful. Fees vary but US rates are 5 per cent for the first million, 4 per cent for the second and 3 per cent thereafter.

Entrepreneurs should be aware that fee for success is riskier for the adviser. However, a successful adviser should gain more reward. Entrepreneurs should also be aware that investment bankers will sometimes ask for both time-based charges and a fee for success. A common method is to work on a 'best efforts' basis combined with share options. 'Best efforts' represent an effort and not a result. Paying someone a fee for a 'best effort' should be resisted, particularly if the effort is not defined.

Entrepreneurs should also treat options with care, although they can be a most useful weapon when raising finance. Most entrepreneurs do not realise options have both an intrinsic value and a time value. The intrinsic value is easy to understand—it is the difference between the buy-in price of the option and actual price per share. For example if you have an option to buy shares at $1.00 (known as the strike price) and the present price is $1.50, then the option has an intrinsic value of 50c. The time value is more difficult to define. As an indication of the time value one can look at the Exchange Traded Options in the newspaper. The value of an option varies according to many factors, including interest rates, share price expectations, share price volatility, time to expiry date, and the ratio of current price to strike price. Options have a time value. Typically this will gradually erode as the option expiry date draws nearer, declining steeply in the final months. As an example of option value, take the price of an Exchange Traded Option for a share whose strike and current price were identical. The value of the option depended purely on the time to expiry (see Table 16.1). For every month beyond three months the option price increased by 1 per cent, and for a three-month option the price is around 10 per cent. All too often entrepreneurs give away options when they should act as another source of funds.

Till now we have been discussing how to raise equity capital

Table 16.1   An example of option value

Time to expiry of option	Percentage of current price
2 months	8.3%
5 months	12.7%
8 months	15.7%

for a high-growth company. Raising money for a management buy-out uses many of the same principles, but is complicated by the greater number of players. Typically you have the vendor, the management, equity investors, debt lenders and mezzanine investors. For a management buy-out you almost certainly want a financial adviser. However, to maintain credibility your adviser should also invest some equity in the buy-out.

The tax and financing aspects of buy-outs are complex and legislation affecting buy-outs in Australia is constantly being modified. It is critical for a buy-out that the structuring be done in the most tax-effective manner. Furthermore, during a buy-out, because of the number of different parties, allegiances keep changing. Negotiations are similar to the diplomatic negotiations which occur when the state and federal governments meet for the annual Premiers' Conference. Management may agree with the vendors that the warranties required by the investors are too strict, and the next day side with the institutional investors against the lenders, who maintain that debt/equity ratios of the proposed structure are too high.

Negotiations are a complex process. The time spent on them and the stress they engender should not be underestimated. But initial sound negotiations followed by good documentation will reduce the negotiating load during later rounds of investment.

PART IV

INVESTING THE MONEY—WHAT INVESTORS MUST DO

17 Screening criteria and due diligence

In the second half of this book we examine the task of the venture capital investors. This and the next four chapters follow a single deal through the investment cycle. The venture capital investment cycle goes through five stages:

- screening and due diligence
- valuation
- structuring and completion
- post investment activities
- exiting.

In this part of the book we devote an individual chapter to each stage. The last part of the book deals with the investor who is managing a portfolio of venture capital investments.

Screening criteria

Chapter 2 advised entrepreneurs to analyse a market by remembering the economists' dictum of keeping one eye on demand and the other eye on supply. Similarly, venture capitalists should keep one eye on buying and the other eye on selling. Unfortunately, most non-professional (and many professional) investors develop a squint and prefer the excitement of purchasing and spending money to the strain of selling.

Many commentators regard the late Larry Adler of FAI as one of the most astute investors in Australia. He had a particular reputation for picking takeover targets. He never made any secret of his formula for success. Instead of examining a target and trying to establish if the current market valuation was lower than some intrinsic valuation, he tried to establish whether there was another potential purchaser of the company in the market. If he could envisage one or more potential purchasers of the company, he bought first. Venture capitalists should adopt a similar perspective.

Successful real estate investors adopt the same philosophy. What the oft-quoted rule 'location, location, location' means is that the most common objection a potential buyer has to a property is its location. Location is a knockout emotional objection. While a seller can overcome many other objections, poor location is almost impossible. All the seller can do is wait for buyers for whom location is not a major issue, and those buyers are few. Otherwise they may start dropping the price to widen the potential market and compensate for the objection.

Venture capital investors, therefore, should examine their investment in terms of potential buyers. The two most rewarding takeout mechanisms for the venture capital investor are the stock market and the corporate investor. As a general rule the venture capital investor will get a greater return from the stock market. While both techniques are examined in more detail in the chapter on exit mechanisms, the simplest rule to remember is that both groups want profits, and preferably a profit after tax of at least $1 million.

It follows that the first question venture capitalists should ask is whether the proposed investment can generate $1 million in profit after tax in a reasonable time (say, between three and seven years). The investment task then becomes twofold. First, venture capitalists should carry out an initial screening to establish whether the business can reach $1 million in post-tax profits. If the answer is positive, the second stage, known as due diligence, establishes the risk of failure.

The first stage of initial screening is to meet the entrepreneur and read the business plan. Investors are then like salespeople after the first cold call on a prospect. They must qualify the prospect to try to establish whether it is worth meeting again. When I was a salesman I was taught to qualify prospects using the acronym MAN, which led me to ask the following questions:

- Does the prospect have the Money to buy the product?
- Does the prospect have the Authority to buy the product?
- Does the prospect have a Need for the product?

Investors should have a similar grid or questionnaire to screen deals. One way is to use the simple mnemonic MAMECH to help you remember how to qualify an investment prospect.

- Market size
- Advantage
- Management team
- Endorsements
- Capital requirements
- History.

Market size

If the market is too small then no matter what happens the company will never be able to produce the necessary profit. As a rough rule of thumb, it is impossible to generate profits of $1 million plus from a market smaller than $50 million. Within five years it will be difficult to build a market share greater than 20 per cent and net profits after tax rarely exceed 10 per cent. Microsoft, the supplier of PC-DOS for the IBM Personal Computer and MS-DOS for the PC clones, receives a royalty for software on every IBM PC sold. Its highest annual net margin was 22 per cent. It is difficult to conceive of a better margin business. If the potential market is less than $50 million, venture capitalists should pass. On the other hand, if the potential market is large the investment becomes increasingly attractive.

Advantage

The next question is what is the significant competitive advantage of the business? Normally the advantage is some product or technology edge, but there may be others, such as a new method of marketing. It helps if the technological edge is proprietary. As mentioned earlier, protection provided by patent is limited. Products protected by design, copyright, or confidentiality agreements are preferred. It is useful to have an accurate costing of the research and development. Generally R&D represents 1–3 per cent of the total turnover of a product. Take a product that is projected to have annual sales in the next eight years of say $1, 3, 6, 10, 10, 6, 3, 1 million, or $40 million in total. Between $400 000 and $1.2 million should have been spent on R&D. If not, there is probably an inconsistency in the product sales projections.

Management team

The management team is the next variable. Typically the team will consist of an entrepreneurial leader and several managers. Entrepreneurs come in all shapes and sizes. A helpful book, *Australia's New Entrepreneurs,* compiled by Anne Fox and published by Enterprise Australia Publications, tells the stories of eleven Australian entrepreneurs. The final chapter of the book, entitled 'The Common Thread', tries to provide an answer to the question 'What makes a successful entrepreneur?'.

One common characteristic of successful entrepreneurs is an abundance of energy, which can best be gauged by meeting them. Another characteristic is persistence. Again and again entrepreneurs have overcome obstacles by a combination of persistence and rat-like cunning. Gauging persistence can be done by asking entrepreneurs to tell their stories, asking them about lessons they have learnt and mistakes they have made. These will all provide clues.

Another characteristic of entrepreneurs is fluency. Business plans are valuable to investors because they show something of how well the entrepreneur can communicate. If entrepreneurs cannot communicate with investors, how can they communicate with customers and employees?

The final characteristic of entrepreneurs described in the book is the ability to set realistic goals and achieve them. Nearly all the entrepreneurs followed the management axiom of planning the work and then working the plan. Most admitted that events modified the original plan and goals changed. Nevertheless, conscious goal-setting was a common thread.

While gauging the energy level, persistence, fluency, and goal-setting capability of an entrepreneur is difficult and subjective, it is possible to measure his or her financial commitment. There is debate among venture capitalists as to whether the commitment should be everything or substantial but there is no doubt it should be significant. If investors do not see a financial commitment from the entrepreneur that represents a significant part of his or her assets (known in the game as 'hurt money') they should wonder if the investment will succeed.

The entrepreneur is a key part of any deal but no entrepreneur can walk alone. It is difficult to gauge the quality of a management team but within the organisation should be people assigned to carry out the business functions of marketing, operations, and administration.

Endorsements

The next step is to deduce from the plan the quality of approvals the company and the concept have received. Some endorsements are better than others. Support accompanied by the receipt of money, such as a sale to a large customer or investment by a reputable institution, is better than an expert's report obtained by payment of fees. The best endorsement is one given by a large technically competent buyer who has bought the product. A qualified investor who has invested equity in the project provides another good endorsement. If neither is available, venture capitalists must look to other endorsements. Again, the quality of these can vary. Future investors are happier if a successful and respected businessperson is either a director or, preferably, a non-executive chairman. On the other hand, it has been my experience that technical and market research reports by experts have limited value. Unfortunately, as many investors in the 1986–87 high-technology floats have realised, the predictions of experts often fail to occur. Many experts have only limited knowledge of the marketplace in which the company operates. Reports prepared by management consultants or auditors tend to have the same defect.

Capital requirements

The next step is to establish whether the capital requirements of the business are reasonable and within the investors' limits It is important to establish exactly how much entrepreneurs need and in what form. Investors should be sensitive to the total amount of capital exposure. As a rule Australian entrepreneurs tend to underestimate the funds required.

History

Finally, investors should have in mind the history of the company. The company should provide the latest copy of the accounts with the business plan. Failure to do so is suspicious. A business history of persistence, innovative marketing campaigns and a fierce dedication to controlling costs are signals of a good investment.

After one meeting and a skim of the business plan, investors should be able to reject the plan or decide that the company is worth further investigation. The finance industry describes the further examination as due diligence. The most common true reasons for rejection are:

- The market is too small.
- The market is large but the company has insufficient competitive advantage.
- The entrepreneur/management team is inadequate.
- The capital requirement is too small.
- The pre-funding valuation by the entrepreneur is too high.

Other reasons, such as not investing in start-ups or not investing in your industry, are excuses. Entrepreneurs would be justified in demanding the real reason.

Valuation, the subject of the next chapter, is the one variable it is possible to change. Valuation is a movable feast. Investors should wait for entrepreneurs to value the company first in the small hope of undervaluation. Once this valuation is given, there is no reason for investors not to reply back with their own estimate without prejudice. It is rare for an entrepreneur to value his or her company less than an investor does. When this does occur it is typically the investor who is later proven wrong.

If venture capitalists do consider a proposal worthwhile they should draft an internal paper on the proposal using the headings above. The completed document should be looked at again the next day. If it still looks good, the next step is to proceed to due diligence. Venture capitalists employed by a venture capital company would distribute the paper among their colleagues, who would discuss the proposition and jointly establish whether they should go on with due diligence.

Due diligence

Investing is a trade-off between risk and reward. The reward side of the equation depends on the valuation and structure of the deal, which are covered in the next two chapters. Due diligence establishes the riskiness of an investment.

There are five risks investors should analyse when carrying out due diligence:

- development,
- manufacturing,
- market,
- management, and
- financing risks.

The information required to establish these risks comes from a variety of sources and typically takes at least a man-month of effort to collect. It will usually take two months in chronological time to complete the due diligence task.

Development risk

Development risk is the risk that no product, only 'vapourware', will be or has been developed. Contrary to the popular notion, venture capitalists rarely invest in products yet to be developed. A statement such as 'I need $1 million dollars to prove the concept' will send venture capitalists ducking for cover. There are occasional exceptions to the rule, but they are rare and should represent no more than 5 per cent of a venture capitalist's portfolio. Entrepreneurs in start-up mode may raise funds from three sources: the public sector, large corporations who are looking for marketing rights, or wealthy individuals, known as 'angels', who look upon the investment as a combination of tax loss and pleasure. What may attract an Australian venture capitalist is a proposal with an exceptional management team, large market potential and substantial commitment of government funding.

Venture capitalists must try to establish whether there is a potential outside development that will prevent the company making a target post-tax profit of $1 million. If the significant competitive advantage of the company is based on technology, investors should ask independent experts. While technical or academic experts may be helpful, a better alternative is to try to contact recently retired chief executives in the industry. Because of their experience these individuals have a wealth of information about the market and product development cycles. Moreover, they think in strategic terms and can often provide useful insights about the industry. While it is difficult to try to predict the technological future for a company, investors should try to obtain a history of product developments for the past ten years. Typically product cycles range from three to five years on release to the market.

Venture capitalists will usually require, at minimum, a working prototype installed on trial at a customer's site. If, however, they decide to invest in research and development it is worth remembering some statistics. For the period 1979–1985 the federal government funded a number of large scale R & D projects under a scheme known as the Section 39 Public Interest Program. The program invested $53.6 million across 29 projects. The program initiators, concerned that public funding would result in commercial success and possibly enrich companies, biased the program towards projects which were in the public interest. Nevertheless, several astute entrepreneurs arranged funding of some major projects which developed into successful businesses. The program was later the subject of a report which noted among other things that the typical project took twice as long as originally estimated and overshot the cost budget by about 33 per cent. The common reasons for the delay were the inability to either recruit the right staff or get necessary equipment.

Manufacturing risk

If the company has developed a prototype, the next step is to establish whether it can commercially produce the product. For companies based on life sciences such as biotechnology or aquaculture, the reason for rejection is often excessive manufacturing risk. Even the most experienced farmers have crop failures due to poor weather or disease.

A similar problem occurs with companies based around a new form of advertising. The entrepreneur may have invented a sign which uses new technology such as holograms or computers. The profits, based on the number of advertisers who will flock to use the new medium, look terrific. Unfortunately, the company is unable to obtain sites on which to place the advertisements.

Another manufacturing risk is risk of supply. Electronics companies in Australia have a problem finding inexpensive components. Investors should establish whether there are any critical components supplied only by a single source. Another problem in Australia is the supply of certain types of labour. Cheap and illegal Mexican labour has built Silicon Valley. There are few chip plants around Boston.

Government restrictions or legal changes are another risk. Investors must obtain warranties or proof if they are investing in a manufacturing business that the necessary government approvals have been secured or may be secured without difficulty. Government restrictions in Australia, while not onerous, are numerous and compliance is expensive. Similar difficulties arise when trying to export electronics and communications products overseas.

When venture capitalists will bear manufacturing risk is when there is a guaranteed market. For many commodity and primary produce products the market is definite and the selling costs are minimal. If you can produce the product you can sell it. Even so, investors should understand the dynamics of the market, especially the price history. Moreover, once the manufacturing facility is built, the company should be the low-cost producer. As an example, CSR can produce sugar at 4c a pound. No matter what happens it is the world's low-cost producer and it can usually make a profit in times of over-supply and depressed prices.

Even if the company is manufacturing the product, investors still need to do due diligence. They should take the bill of materials for two or three major products, establish the product cost, and then calculate the gross margin. If the gross margin is below 50 per cent it is unlikely the company will produce adequate profits. Good manufacturing businesses have gross profit margins of over 50 per cent and successful investments have margins of between 60 per cent and 80 per cent.

Marketing risk

Venture capitalists prefer not to bear either development or manufacturing risk. They do expect to bear the market and management risks. The marketing risk is the risk that there will be inadequate sales for the product. Among the key issues investors should address are the size, growth, and expected market share of the company.

Entrepreneurs are by nature optimistic and their optimism is reflected in the way they perceive the size of the potential market and the potential market share. The size of a market and its growth rate are usually difficult to establish and investors must spend time trying to ascertain both figures independently.

One problem with Australia is that the market statistics are limited. On the other hand, the US keeps comprehensive statistics and sometimes a guess may be made by interpolation. For example, if you know that annual US frozen yogurt consumption is 3.62 kilograms per capita, you may estimate the total potential Australian market as 16 × 3.62 or 58 million kilograms. Government studies, particularly Industries Assistance Commission (IAC) reports, are another source of information. The IAC reports, while they are principally arguments for lowering tariffs in an industry, usually contain a comprehensive industry analysis. In addition, the reports generally list the major competitors and experts in the industry.

Another public source of information is the import/export statistics. These are obtained by a visit to the Australian Bureau of Statistics. Currency fluctuations may distort the figures but they still provide a useful guide to the size and growth rate of a market. The statistics are comprehensive and reasonably timely.

Industry associations may also provide estimates of market size. Secretaries of associations can provide a wealth of information about the industry and should be contacted. Secretaries are often familiar with the entrepreneurs in an industry and can provide independent corroboration of many details.

Another source of information is the media. The easiest way to access the media is to use a computerised search facility. There are now companies which prepare abstracts of articles and books and then load the abstracts into computers. By entering a key word and time period, users can obtain a listing of article abstracts for the subject. After reading the abstracts they can then choose those articles they think will be of interest.

Customers are another source of corroboration. Investors should talk to at least six customers and establish their views about the product and the company. Talking to customers should also help establish the competition, the buying criteria, the reputation of the entrepreneur, and so on. Another tip for investors is to write out a summary immediately after a telephone interview. If not, they will find later interviews will overwrite it in memory.

There are several other characteristics of markets that venture capitalists like to see besides size (greater than $100 million) and growth (greater than 20 per cent a year). One is low promotional costs. High advertising costs are a barrier to entry, causing immediate difficulty. Products advertised widely by word of mouth have a greater likelihood of success. Products or services that do not require advertising are preferred because they do not attract competition so easily. Take, for example, the first wine coolers. While the early starters gained large market share, over 40 competitive products appeared within six months.

Venture capitalists also prefer many competent buyers who are homogeneous. It is important to market a basic, easy-to-use product which, if necessary, can be simply and easily tailored by the customer. Products that require substantial after-sales service or tailoring usually result in marginally profitable companies. An ideal product/market nexus is an item that retails for around $2000 to industrial buyers and includes some element of repeat business. Good examples would be modems, facsimile machines, cellular telephones, and bottled spring-water coolers.

Finally there should not be any significant institutional barriers to sales. Examples of such barriers are Underwriting Laboratory approval in the US for electronic goods, drug approvals by the Department of Health, or Austel approvals for communications networks.

When analysing a market, investors should distinguish between flows and stock. Tourism, for example, comprises travel to and from the destination and activity while there. For carriers such as airlines the crucial measure of the market is flow. For hotels the size of the market depends on the stock of visitors. The stock is the average flow multiplied by the average length of stay. The flow is easy to measure and length of stay may be obtained by survey. This leads to anomalies, such as the flow of Japanese tourists to Australia and Australian visitors to Europe being roughly the same but the stock of Australian visitors in Europe being five times greater. Thus many hotels which are being justified on the basis of increased tourism flows will probably be initially unprofitable because of low stock.

One key to business success is to convert the revenue from a once-off stock sale into a regular cash flow. The Chep pallets division of Brambles is a good example of this technique. Pallets could be sold from stock but by renting them Brambles obtains an even and steady cash flow.

Once investors have decided on the size of the market they can take the sales projections in the business plan and calculate the market share. A first-year market share greater than 1–2 per cent and a market share within three years of greater than 10 per cent are danger signs. Companies do not gain 25 per cent market share in three years. If they do the market is generally too small.

Management risk

Management risk is the risk that even though product may be manufactured and sold no profits will be made. Again, the best technique of establishing this risk is the interview. Ask the entrepreneur for at least six references. The selection is usually informative. After asking referees how long they have known the individual and how often they meet, the real interview starts. The key questions to ask are:

- What are the entrepreneur's three strongest characteristics?
- Does the entrepreneur have a track record of making profits in the industry?
- Can you relate any experiences where the entrepreneur showed persistence and originality in overcoming problems?
- How does the entrepreneur perform under stress?
- What do you think are the entrepreneur's goals in life?
- How well does the entrepreneur manage other people?
- Does the entrepreneur finish projects or leave them incomplete?
- Would you have any doubts about the entrepreneur's integrity?
- Would you invest in the business if you were given the opportunity?
- Who else knows the individual and could give me a reference?

In addition you should also do a credit check on the company and its directors by using a well-known agency such as Dun & Bradstreet.

What you are trying to discover is if the entrepreneur and his or her associates have the combination of drive, intelligence and persistence to succeed. Investors should have their antennae ready to detect any signs of lack of integrity. If there is the slightest doubt about integrity you must walk away from the deal. It is doubtful whether the referees supplied by entrepreneurs will provide an indication about integrity, but friends of friends often do. The credit-checking agencies are another source of information and must be used. About one deal in twenty has a whiff of scam about it. What distinguishes the professional investor from the amateur is not so much the ability to pick winners but the ability to minimise losses.

It has been my experience with references that the entrepreneur either checks out well or a feeling of doubt begins to develop and then becomes stronger. It is rarely a marginal case. The market and technology can seduce investors, who then disregard lukewarm approval. They may not bother to check references. But they should obtain positive endorsement from the reference-checking and not 50/50 statements.

The best reference of all is track record. People who have been successful and made money for investments or employers tend to be able to repeat the process. What investors like to see is an entrepreneur who has gained experience as a general manager for a profit centre of a multinational corporation. He or she should know about performing to budgets, reducing costs and generating sales and profits, and have developed management skills.

Financing risks

Financing risk is the risk that when the injected funds are used up, the company will be unable to raise further funds. As stated earlier, the venture capital game regards fund-raising as an annual event. The financing risk may be estimated in several ways. If the cash burn needed to develop the product or build the factory is faster than projected, the equity raised may be used up too quickly. Also sales may occur later than projected. Finally, either the variable or fixed expenses may be underestimated.

The first task for venture capitalists is to produce on a personal computer their own cash flow model of the investment using a spreadsheet. They should use a spreadsheet with graphics capability; then they can play around with the model, increasing the expenses, lagging the sales, and so on. They should develop their own sensitivity analysis for the company. For example, each month the launch is delayed will cost $30 000. By using a cumulative cash flow graph, investors, can develop a feel for the realism of the entrepreneur's projections.

The next task is to produce pro-forma balance sheets and income statements, and then calculate key ratios. Investors should first calculate the after-tax and gross margins. Far too many business plans contain ridiculous estimates of net profit margins. Figures over 10 per cent for after-tax margins are likely to be over-optimistic. Expenses as a percentage of sales should also be calculated. R & D should be 5–10 per cent, administration should be 8–10 per cent, and marketing expenses should be 10–25 per cent.

The next set of ratios calculated should be the capital turn ratios. Manufacturers rarely obtain capital turn ratios in excess of three, wholesalers seldom beat five. Debtors typically run 60 to 75 sales-days, as does stock. Also, the debt/equity ratios should be calculated to see if the company is overgeared. As a general principle total debt should not be greater than net tangible assets. Finally the ratio of pre-interest cash flow to interest payments should be calculated. As a rule a growing company should have a buffer of at least twice the interest payment.

Finally, investors should calculate the sales/employee ratio. The poor business plan generally contains too many people at the beginning and too few people at the end. A good target figure for the sales/employee ratio for a manufacturer is between $120 000 and $140 000, while a wholesaler's should be twice that.

After the cash flow and ratio analysis the final tool of financial analysis is breakeven analysis. The calculations have been discussed in Chapter 13. One good test of entrepreneurs is to see if they have calculated the breakeven point for their business. What is important for investors is to calculate the desired income point, which is the amount of sales required to generate a desired income. The formula for calculating the desired income point is:

$$\text{Desired income point} = \frac{(\text{fixed costs} + \text{desired income})}{\text{contribution ratio}}$$

For most businesses the variable costs are few. For example, in a restaurant the variable costs are food, drink and credit card charges. Investors must establish accurate fixed costs and then determine what prices will be necessary to achieve the desired income. Many new businesses often price their services or products too low. On the other hand, if the market is one with a high degree of price sensitivity then investors could have problems.

Investors need to be comfortable with the funds required and how they are going to be used. They should then try to establish the profits and performances of the company in one year's time in the event everything goes to plan and in the event of things going wrong. Then a valuation for the company can be developed, using the techniques discussed in the next chapter. From the projected valuation investors should then establish the risk of not being able to raise further funds.

Once investors have established the risks involved in a project they can balance the risks against the estimated reward. As general rule investors should not accept more than two risks in an investment. Any more is likely to lead to capital loss.

18 Valuation

Once venture capitalists decide the investment proposal will serve a sufficiently large market, has significant competitive advantage, and at minimum has a competent and commercial entrepreneur, they must value the proposition. When deciding on the valuation the investors must distinguish between the post-funding and pre-funding valuations. The difference is best described by an example. Assume a company with 100 000 issued shares decides to make a new issue of 20 000 shares at $50 a share to raise $1 million. Then the post-funding valuation is 120 000 x $50, or $6 million; the pre-funding valuation is 100 000 x $50, or $5 million.

Another way is to calculate the post-funding valuation by percentages and then deduct the cash remaining in the company to calculate the pre-funding valuation. For example, if an investor, after an investment of $1 000 000 cash, which remains in the company, owns 40 per cent of the voting capital then the post-funding valuation is $1 million/0.4, or $2.5 million. The pre-funding valuation is then $2.5 million less $1 million, or $1.5 million. If, on the other hand, 50 per cent of the cash 'leaves the ring', then the pre-funding valuation increases to $2 million.

Many inexperienced entrepreneurs fail to recognise the difference between pre-funding and post-funding valuations, which can be useful during negotiations. Many do not either look at the value of their company or think in terms of share price. They tell themselves they do not want to give up more than 40 per cent of the company and the company needs $2 million. Thus they fix the value implicitly, even though it has no bearing on reality.

Entrepreneurs should ask themselves what their company is really worth before an injection of funds. Even better is to think in terms of share price. For example, if a company has 150 000 shares on issue and its board considers the current share price to be $3.25, the company is valued at $487 500. As the company grows and funds are injected annually, the entrepreneur and other members of the management team are cognisant of the need to increase the share price and to do so in a commercially appealing fashion.

Indeed, entrepreneurs may use this approach to advantage. One Australian entrepreneur after every injection of equity automatically raises the share price by 50 per cent and only accepts minimum parcels of $500 000. In the same way some US venture capitalists will not invest on principle at a share price greater than 400 per cent of the last purchase price.

This way of calculating the pre-funding valuation will help venture capitalists in negotiations with entrepreneurs involved in start-ups or where the company has a limited history of sales or earnings. It is difficult to put a pre-funding valuation greater than $500 000 on any start-up, unless entrepreneurs are able to put on the table their own money, or money from other invest-ors or government schemes.

Another rule the Australian venture capital investor should consider adopting is not investing in high-growth deals at a pre-funding valuation greater than $10 million. Higher valua-tions should only apply to companies that are near to a public listing. A valuation greater than $10 million is usually too high and probably has inadequate growth potential to justify the risk involved.

On the other hand, the valuation for a leveraged buy-out should be considerably higher. Assume the exit mechanism for a leveraged buy-out is predicated to be a public offering. If the minimum valuation acceptable to institutions is $20 million, the leveraged buy-out valuation should be similar. Both investors and entrepreneurs should note as a general rule that in a leveraged buy-out investors should pay no more than seven times Earnings Before Interest and Taxation (EBIT) and aim at a valuation of five times EBIT. As the EBIT for a mature company is usually 7–10 per cent of sales, the minimum range of turnover for a leveraged buy-out is between $28 million and $40 million.

The public stock market has established several ways of valuing a company which apply to private company investment. Nevertheless there are some important differences to consider in tandem with the methods of valuation.

The first way to value a company is to use its net worth (assets less liabilities) and then adjust for undervalued or undisclosed assets. This approach is most commonly used to value investment or real estate companies and should be used to value a leveraged buy-out. For any investment, an investor must always calculate the net assets per share, net tangible assets per share, and the price-to-book-value ratio.

Many people dismiss asset valuations for high-growth companies as irrelevant. On the other hand, many new companies include intangible assets on their balance sheet. One class of intangible asset is the revalued asset. Typically the revalued asset is either a revaluation of intellectual property or a marketing licence. From the asset revaluation it used to be possible in Australia to issue bonus shares to the existing shareholders. Such issues are no longer possible, but the revaluations are still done to try to add value to a company. As the board of directors carrying out the revaluation and entrepreneurs seeking funds at the highest valuation are often closely associated, any investor should treat such revaluations with caution.

The other form of asset revaluation is to capitalise research and development or product launch expenses. This practice has the double effect of reducing expenses in the profit and loss account and building up the asset side of the balance sheet. As R & D is a future benefit, some argue it should be taken out of future sales. It is similar to the justification property developers sometimes use to capitalise interest on a mortgage on the grounds that it will be recovered when the building is sold. The countervailing view is to account conservatively, accept the bad news early and the good news when it happens. Interest rates may compound faster than the capital growth of the land. Professional institutional equity-investment managers prefer the latter principle and automatically remove intangible assets unless there is a history of profits and sales as justification. Examples of acceptable intangible assets are newspaper mastheads and longstanding brand names. Venture capitalists and private investors should follow the professionals.

If the price-to-book ratio is greater than 1 or the net assets contain significant intangibles then the investor must demand justification. They can turn the asset valuation method to advantage. They should calculate the pre-funding valuation, subtract the net tangible worth of the company and ask the entrepreneur to justify the difference. The difference can only be one of two asset types: identifiable intangibles, and a residual amount, commonly called goodwill, which comprises unidentifiable intangible assets. What value you put on identifiable intangibles is a matter of contention. However, let us take the extreme example of an invention which will attract a licence fee of 2.5 per cent and whose expected annual sales will be worth $1 million. The life of such a product will be ten years, which in today's environment is a long product cycle. If we apply a discount rate of 12 per cent, then the net present value of the licence is $141 255. Few products achieve $10 million in total sales. Thus when one sees licence revaluations of several millions in new companies, the directors, probably unintentionally, are implying sales of several tens of millions. When trying to establish the value of an intangible asset, ask who would really pay that value for the asset. Is it transferable? How long will the intangible asset hold its value? Patents, for example, have a limited lifespan and are only of value if the holder has the power to fight the infringer in court.

The most common valuation technique used by investment analysts for industrial stocks is the price–earnings ratio (commonly known as the P/E ratio). One calculates the P/E ratio in two steps. First calculate the market capitalisation of a company by multiplying the number of ordinary shares on issue by the last sale price for a share. Then divide the market capitalisation by the total earnings due to the ordinary shares on issue. Earnings due to shareholders are generally defined as profits after tax. Implicit in the P/E ratio is the assumption that earnings will be maintainable over that period or will substantially increase. For example a company with a net profit of $1 million on a P/E of 10 is expected to earn a similar figure for at least the next ten years.

Investors should be aware of several traps with P/E ratios. First, net profit is a post-tax figure. Far too many Australian entrepreneurs show complete ignorance of P/E ratios and apply them to pre-tax figures. Moreover, it is easy to distort the earnings figure. One popular technique is to treat extraordinary profits as ordinary profits. Another method is to use a lower than standard corporate tax rate. When carrying out a valuation the investor should eliminate extraordinary profits such as asset sales and one-off royalties, and profits earned from interest-bearing deposits, and use the normal tax rate. The earnings figure should also be calculated after deducting the payment of any preference dividends and minority interests. If a company does not fully own a subsidiary then it cannot claim 100 per cent of the profit the subsidiary may make. The accounting convention for minority interests is to first claim 100 per cent of earnings and then deduct profit attributable to outside shareholders.

The average P/E ratio for all listed stocks is calculated weekly by the Australian Stock Exchange and published each Monday in the *Australian Financial Review*. It is a useful figure and every investor should be familiar with the current value. Two ratios are published: the All-Ordinaries and All-Industrials. The Australian Stock Eschange has a higher proportion of resource stocks than most stock exchanges. Resource stocks tend to be price takers and fluctuating commodity prices dominate the profits. The P/E ratios for mining stocks tend to be volatile. The All-Ordinaries P/E ratio has varied from a low of 6.5 in 1979 to a high of 18.4 in October 1987. For rough calculations the average All-Ordinaries P/E commonly used is 12. Figure 18.1 shows the P/E ratios for the last ten years.

While the publicly listed All-Ordinaries ratio is important, it cannot be applied indiscriminately to private companies. First, the All-Ordinaries P/E ratio contains a premium for liquidity. As many stock market investors found to their cost the eventual

Figure 18.1 P/E ratios for the past ten years

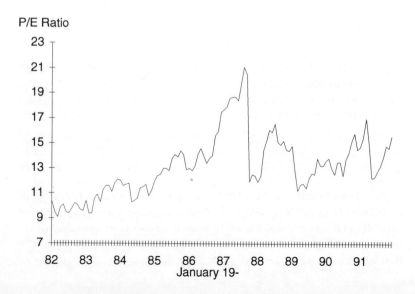

P/E Ratio

January 19-

selling price of second-line stocks after the October 1987 crash resulted in P/Es about half those of the blue chips. Second, the market requires a company to prove itself and develop a history of improving earnings. A newly listed stock is not brought to the market at a P/E equal to the All-Ordinaries ratio but at a discount, typically of about one-third. To incorporate these two factors of limited liquidity and lack of earnings history, investors must discount the All-Ordinaries P/E ratio by about two-thirds for private companies. In 1979 investors in a private company should have used a P/E of about 2 while, at the height of the 1987 boom, they should have used a P/E of around 7.

The problem with using P/Es with many private or newly started companies is there are no profits. Two approaches have been developed in the US: to use either an estimate of future earnings or a price-to-revenue ratio.

The price-to-revenue ratio is an easy multiple to understand (it is the ratio of market capitalisation to annual operating revenues) and is a common calculation for publicly listed stocks in the US. As a rule US investors look to buy on price/revenue ratios of around 50 per cent and would regard a ratio of 300 per cent as a maximum. The earnings/sales ratio varies between about 3 per cent and 8 per cent for most industrial companies. These ratios imply a minimum P/E ratio of 4 to 12 and a maximum ratio of between 37.5 and 100. The private company investor who uses the price-to-revenue ratio technique should aim at a ratio of one-third and not pay more than 100 per cent of revenue.

The estimate of future earnings approach is probably the most common method described in the venture capital textbooks. The calculation involves taking an earnings figure in, say, three to four years time, multiplying it by some price/earnings ratio and then discounting the value back to a net present value. Investors using this method must make three decisions.

- What P/E ratio should be used?
- What discount rate should be used?
- What time period should be used?

The prevailing interest rates and the stage of the investment combine to determine the discount rate. Interest rates over the last ten years have shown as much fluctuation as equity prices, as Figure 18.2 illustrates. What the investor must do is use a market-sensitive long-term rate. The easiest to use is the ten-

year Commonwealth bond rate, which is published in the financial section of most major newspapers. The question then
becomes which multiple to apply to this interest rate. The
multiple must vary according to the stage of the business. Using
the definitions stated earlier in the book, there are three precise
stages in the growth of a company.

Stage	Description	Sales	Profits	Multiple
I	Seed/start-up	no	no	4-5
II	Second stage	yes	no	3-4
III	Development	yes	yes	2-3

The gross multiple is then varied according to size of market,
significant competitive advantage and quality of management
team.

The second decision is in which year to apply the P/E ratio.
Earlier in the book we set as a screening criterion whether the
business was capable of earning $1 million post tax. The year
this occurs is the time to apply the P/E ratio. However, the $1
million in net profit must be based on a fully applied tax rate
and should not be when the profit figure is favourably distorted
by carried-forward tax losses. Hence the year chosen will typically be when the pre-tax operating profit is $1.6 million.

Let us now look at three examples, which were calculated
in early 1988. The All-Ordinaries P/E ratio was around 12 so

Figure 18.2 Ten-year bond rate for the past ten years

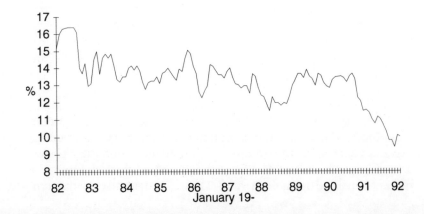

the applied P/E ratio was 4. The ten-year Commonwealth bond rate was around 12 per cent.

Case 1

Start-up company seeking $500 000 which projects earnings of $1.5 million in five years. Market is large, advantage is average, management team is excellent. Apply a discount multiple of 4.5, giving a discount rate of 54 per cent. Then value in five years is 4 times 1.5, or $6 million. 1.54 raised to the fifth power is 8.65. Net present value of $6 million discounted at 54 per cent over five years is $0.69 million, so $500 000 should buy 72 per cent.

Case 2

Second stage company seeking $1 million, projecting $1.25 million earnings in three years. Market is average, advantage is significant, management team is average. Apply a discount multiple of 3.3, or 40 per cent. Then value in three years is 4 times 1.25 or $5 million. 1.4 raised to third power is 2.74. Net present value of $5 million discounted at 40 per cent over three years is $1.82 million, so $1 million should buy 55 per cent.

Case 3

Development stage company seeking $1 million, projecting $1 million net profits in two years. Market is average, advantage is significant, management team is good. Apply a discount multiple of 2, or 24 per cent. Value in two years is 4 times $1 million, or $4 million. 1.24 raised to second power is 1.54. Net present value of $4 million discounted at 24 per cent over two years is $2.6 million, so $1 million should buy 38 per cent.

The third method of valuation is to use comparable company results or industry standards. In many industries there are rules of thumb such as multiples of weekly revenues for restaurants, multiples of litres pumped for gas stations, $X per phone for cellular telephone companies, and so on. Unfortunately many of these multiples are only available for stable industries and the ratios generally favour the seller. Many entrepreneurs often quote US figures. These are figures for listed companies, which as noted before will be about three times the value for a private company. Also the size of the US market reduces the business risk. Industry standards have limited appeal as a valuation method for the private company investor.

While all these forms of financial valuation are in the venture capital books, venture capitalists often use a different approach. To offset the risk of the investment, they look for high returns. Typical expectations are five times the original investment in three years or ten times the original investment in five years. These objectives equate to compound growth rates of 71 per cent and 58 per cent respectively. Venture capitalists also realise the fund-raising never stops and each year brings a new injection of equity. Hence the method they most commonly use is to try to establish the value for the company in the next fund-raising or when there will be an exit. Venture capitalists try to guess the exit price and work backwards. They try to estimate the amount of each capital raising. The share price should rise by 50 per cent to 75 per cent at each round of fund-raising. There is an example of this approach in Chapter 6, 'How the Game is Played'.

All these methods of valuation are valid and will lead to a range of values. Ultimately the investor and entrepreneur must remember that the valuation is the price at which people are willing to invest and it is a subjective figure. If no deal is done, no actual valuation has been achieved. On the other hand, there is one test investors should always apply before investing. Would they be able to turn around and with a reasonable amount of effort sell their newly acquired holding at breakeven or a small profit? If not convinced, then they should not invest.

19 Structuring the deal

If investors decide a proposal is believable and the valuation is such that the rewards outweigh the risks, the next step is to structure the deal. First we shall discuss the objectives of entrepreneurs and the investors, followed by a description of the tools of structuring, and finish with a discussion of other structuring issues investors should address.

Due diligence of the business opportunity and agreeing on the valuation appear to take most time, but the structure of a deal is probably more important. Good business prospects have been ruined by improper structures; similarly, entrepreneurs or investors have not received their just reward from business success because of poor structure.

We have already stated the rules of the venture capital game, but it is important to repeat those relevant to structuring:

- The common objective of both parties is to build an enterprise generating sufficient after-tax profits so the institutions will invest in a public listing.
- Building such an enterprise will require a series of funding injections.
- Dividend imputation, the 150 per cent tax deduction for research and development, and delayed payment of company tax now make the private company the most attractive business organisation.
- The financing task is finding sources of unsecured debt and equity.

The first step in determining the investment structure is to realise that the objectives of investors and entrepreneurs differ. Entrepreneurs' wishes are simple—they wish to give up as little equity for as much cash as possible. Surprisingly, it is a mistake for the investor to take the opposite view and try to get as much equity for as little cash as possible. If the cash amount is too small (and usually entrepreneurs underestimate the cash requirements) then the business stalls because another round of funding must be started. On the other hand, if the business is overcapitalised, entrepreneurs may purchase luxury cars and lease space in expensive offices. Every farmer knows that too much water can kill a crop as surely as too little—the amount of funding is as important as the implied valuation. Secondly, if initial investors take too much equity, later dilutions may result in too little equity residing with the entrepreneurs, who will lose motivation. Venture capital investors should have different goals. They should be seeking the return of their capital with an adequate reward for the risk taken, combined with the ability to share in the gains on an equitable basis with the entrepreneurs if the business becomes a success.

Private investors and entrepreneurs should also carefully evaluate their motives when investing. If investors do not aim to achieve a return by a publicly listed vehicle or if entrepreneurs are uncomfortable with sharing ownership, then both should seek other forms of funding. The private investor can provide a second mortgage, ask for a royalty on sales or even purchase a building and lease it for a minimal rental. These types of investment substantially reduce the gain but significantly reduce the pain.

It is also important to understand that objectives may change over time. The young entrepreneur may come to realise the business will not grow large enough to list publicly and be content to draw a healthy salary, join the Rotary Club, and seek election to the local council. The investor will then own illiquid private shares with no buyer until the incumbent appointee decides to retire.

The enterprise may fail to meet the original projections. Investors then seek capital recovery and need to ensure they regain their investment before the entrepreneur does. Investors should also consider obtaining a note from entrepreneurs undertaking to repay any investment, if not now, then some time in the future. As a matter of principle, entrepreneurs must have some hurt money at stake. Asking them or their family to recognise a future obligation to repay former backers is not unreasonable. Times change, and while one enterprise may fail another may be very successful. On the other hand, investors occasionally find an entrepreneur who has failed in an enterprise but whose creditors or lenders did not lose any money.

Even better, the entrepreneur paid them back even when not obliged to do so. Investors should back such an individual almost without question.

In summary, venture capital investors are not looking to gain as much ownership for as little money as possible. What they are trying to accomplish is capital return, with some capital gain for either indifferent or marginal performance or significant capital gain if the enterprise prospers, while acknowledging the risk that all their capital may disappear. To produce this result venture capital investors may use various tools.

Venture capital financing is mezzanine financing. The term mezzanine financing is best understood by regarding the choice facing the corporate financier as a multi-storey building. Debt financiers in their search for collateral prefer debt to be secured with a fixed charge against a specific company asset. This debt is at the top of the building and is senior to all other payments at the time of liquidation. Beneath the top floor could be a secured lender with a floating charge over assets. Then there may be unsecured lenders, who rank behind the secured lenders if the company goes into liquidation. Often unsecured lending is done by a negative pledge. This refers to certain financial ratios which the company agrees not to breach. The most common ratios used in a negative pledge are gearing and interest cover. Gearing is the ratio of debt to shareholders' funds. Interest cover is the ratio of earnings before interest and tax to interest paid. Typical target values for gearing and interest cover are below 100 per cent and above 3 respectively.

On the bottom floor of the building are the ordinary shareholders. The original shareholders usually subscribe for shares typically at a par value of 50c or $1. Later investors subscribe at a premium depending on the market value of the share, which has no bearing on the par (or as it is sometimes known, the face or nominal) value of the share. Ordinary shares have voting rights plus the right to receive ordinary dividends. Dividends are paid out of the after-tax profit and are usually paid semi-annually. On the stock exchange, where shares are traded, there could be confusion about whether the buyer or seller is entitled to a dividend. The confusion is eliminated by setting an 'ex dividend' date whereby shares traded after that date are 'ex' (without) the dividend, denoted by XD after the share's name. Shares traded before that date are traded 'cum' dividend.

Mezzanine finance refers to financing between the top floors of debt and bottom floors of equity. Hybrid securities and 'Irish equity' are other names. The three most popular forms of hybrid securities are convertible notes, subordinated debt with options and redeemable preference shares.

Convertible notes

Convertible notes, as the name implies, are a loan for a fixed period at a fixed (but possibly floating) rate of interest. The holders of the convertible note have the right to convert it to ordinary shares at specified dates in the future. If the conversion does not occur the loan is paid off at maturity. In order for the company to be able to deduct the interest payments for tax, conversion of the notes cannot occur within two years from the date of issue, but must occur within ten years. The conversion is at any time, at the option of the lenders. The conversion price must be the greater of the par value of the share or 90 per cent of the market price of the shares during a valuation period before the time of issue.

Convertible notes are popular when interest rates are high and there is a bull market. Convertible notes are a cheap source of debt funds, especially if the company share price is selling near or below par. If the shares are selling at a high yield, by issuing a convertible note the company will gain the tax deduction on the interest. Sometimes financiers recommend convertible notes as a form of financing for initial seed capital. Convertible notes are a good financing method for projects which might take several years to be profitable but where the costs and time of development can be predicted with a reasonable degree of certainty. The lower cost to the company during the development stage converts to a higher cost when the project is profitable. However, for this type of project financing (say a building or a mine), experience provides a reasonably good estimate for development costs, so it is easier to calculate the funding requirements.

A convertible note is usually priced at a premium to share price. The premium is usually a function of the running yield of the note less the dividend yield of the share. Typically investors regard a premium of more than twice the net running yield as too high.

For example, assume a company's shares are trading at $2.00

and pay an 8c dividend, so the dividend yield is 4 per cent. Say the company, which is currently paying 15 per cent on bank bills, wishes to refinance with a convertible note paying around 8 per cent. The maximum amount of premium would be twice the net running yield of (9 – 4) per cent or 10 per cent of $2.00, or 20c. Thus the company could expect to raise funds at $2.20 per note, paying an annual coupon of 20c convertible into one ordinary share.

For venture capital funding each company will have different needs and the funding estimates will always be wrong. The essence of venture capital is to raise funds in tranches. The problem with convertible notes is that they deter the financiers for the next round. Debt lenders regard convertible notes as debt and refuse to lend because the gearing ratio will be too high or the interest cover will be too low. On the other hand, equity investors will immediately convert the convertible note to equity, and calculate the earnings per share post-dilution. The equity investors will usually think the convertible noteholders have too sweet a deal and demand a lower price. But convertible notes can be useful in leveraged buy-outs where later fund-raisings are not envisaged.

Subordinated debt/options

The subordinated debt/option combination suffers from the same deficiencies as the convertible note. Major shareholders typically use subordinated debt for fiduciary or other reasons when they do not want or need to take any more equity as an asset but only want to have debt. A good example would be an MIC already at the 50 per cent ownership level of a company needing to inject further funds into an investment.

However, company options can be a most useful form of incentive for both investors and entrepreneurs. A company option is the option to take up (buy) a new share from a company at some future date at a fixed price known as an exercise or strike price. Options are attractive to investors as an equity sweetener. The market typically values long-dated options higher than their worth when calculated by the mathematical formulas. Thus a company can often obtain equity by attaching to a new issue of shares either an option or part of an option as a 'sweetener'. The legal time limit for options is five years. Options should not be free but should be used to raise money. Company options are useful to motivate entrepreneurs and their employees. Options can be tied to the performance of a company. A typical employee share scheme allows the company to issue between 5 and 10 per cent of shares to employees. By issuing options tied to profit performance, investors achieve both the profits to repay their capital and a more equitable split between the investor and entrepreneurs.

A variation on this theme is piggy-back options. A second series of options is attached to an initial series, typically at a strike price 50 per cent to 100 per cent higher than the strike price of the first set. The issue of the second set occurs upon the exercise of the first options and subscription to the new shares.

Preference shares

Because of the difficulties outlined above, the most popular form of venture capital financing is the preference share. Preference shares rank above ordinary shares for claims on assets, earnings and dividends, but below creditors and lenders. Preference shares usually have a fixed dividend rate attached, expressed as a percentage of the par value unless they are participating preference shares, in which case they participate in ordinary dividend distributions.

Corporate financiers have traditionally treated preference shares as a form of pseudo-debt. For companies that were not paying taxes owing to accumulated losses, preference shares were often a cheaper form of borrowing than debt. This was because, while to a company 10 per cent interest on preference capital was cheaper than 12 per cent on debt, the lender as a company would have to pay tax on interest income but dividends would be tax free. In this example, the lending company could obtain 6 per cent post tax if it lent in the form of debt but 10 per cent if it lent in the form of redeemable preference shares. Moreover, the preference shares were usually not convertible to ordinary shares. Thus the restriction placed on listed companies by the Stock Exchange that no more than an additional 10 per cent of a company's issued capital may be subject to private placement in one year unless there is shareholder approval did not apply. Finally, preference shares could only be redeemed by the issue of more ordinary shares, from retained profits or funds in the share premium account. Thus the price for preference shares was often set at a high premium of, say, $10 000 for a $1 share. Redeemable preference share issues by June 1987 exceeded $5 billion.

This capital market has now declined in importance. Redemptions may not now occur till two years after issue. Moreover, dividend imputation has meant franked dividends are more important to the institutional investors.

Venture capital investors consider convertible redeemable preference shares as an excellent instrument. If there is success, the ability to convert to ordinary shares means investors may participate in any public listing. In the event of failure, investors take precedence over entrepreneurs. If the investment becomes a 'living dead', with moderate but insufficient earnings to list, investors can redeem their shares and recover their original capital.

To motivate entrepreneurs to achieve a public listing, venture capitalists use financial incentives. One technique is to attach a high preference dividend to the shares after a period of, say, four years, so that if listing does not happen the company's profit will all go to the investors. Even more attractive to investors is to make the dividend payments cumulative— if a preference dividend payment is missed, the dividend accumulates and is paid when the company has sufficient profits. Another method is for the investors to have attached to their shares a put option to the entrepreneur. The company options discussed earlier were call options (i.e. the holder has the right to buy stock in the future at a fixed price). Put options give the holder the right to sell shares at a certain price. Buyers of put options treat them as an insurance policy. Sellers of put options believe the company value is going to rise continuously, which *a priori* is what entrepreneurs believe.

Another structuring technique is to divide the investment into two or more separate segments. For simplicity, assume the entrepreneurs have the option to redeem one half of the investment at twice the entry price and that the second half is redeemable only by the investors. The entrepreneurs will then try to generate sufficient profits to redeem the first segment, as it will increase their ownership percentage. For example, say a company has 20 000 shares on issue and it raises $1 million by the issue of 10 000 'A' class shares and 10 000 'B' class shares at an issue price of $50 a share. The redemption price of the 'A' class shares is $100. If the entrepreneurs then have the company redeem the 'A' class preference shares, their ownership will move from 50 per cent to 67 per cent.

The advantage of preference shares, particularly if they are convertible, is that corporate financiers regard them as equity rather than debt. This means entrepreneurs can then raise debt finance and obtain government grants, where a common requirement is that any grant given be matched dollar for dollar with equity.

For start-ups there is often a need for staged funding, with the injection of further funds dependent on the results of the previous stage. A fast-growing company may be compared to a mining start-up where, say, $1 million is wanted for a broad exploration of a claim. If a strike occurs, a further $2 million is raised for precise definition of the orebody and project planning. If the body proves suitable for drilling, then $7 million will be needed over two years to start production. If stages I or II produce negative results, the funding stops. The structure often adopted for start-ups is partly paid or contributing shares. In the example above, the company could issue 10 million partly paid shares in annual tranches of 10c, 20c, 35c, and 35c. In a public limited liability company the shareholder must pay the calls, so the financiers invented no liability (NL) companies, whereby shareholders do not need to pay any uncalled amounts.

Partly paid shares are also a way of providing ownership to entrepreneurs. These shares are often entitled to full dividends, but voting power depends on the amount paid on the shares. Then as the company grows and is successful, entrepreneurs and their employees use the dividends to pay out the remainder of their contribution. The problem with partly-paids is that in the event of liquidation the remainder of the unpaid capital could be called up. The way around that problem is to have the partly-paids held by a $2 company which can default.

Earnouts, put options, and redemption tied to profit performance are all important structuring techniques and the investor should use them to the fullest extent. A. Lipper, in his excellent book *Investing in Private Companies*, quoted a typical US guideline whereby if investors put up all the money they should get 100 per cent of the equity. The stake the entrepreneurs ultimately own depends on the speed at which they pay back the investment. Repayment in one year means the entrepreneurs get 80 per cent, two years 60 per cent, three or more 40 per cent. Earnout structures should relate to market conditions and any formula should be tied to market conditions. A valuation based on a P/E of 5 would have appeared high in 1983 and low in 1987. Earnouts may be structured either by the redemption of preference shares or by the issue of new contributing shares. Astute entrepreneurs sometimes reverse the earnout mechanism to a giveback. In this structure, if the entrepreneurs fail to perform they give up equity. The problem with an equity giveback is that the investors end up owning more of a lemon.

As indicated in Chapter 16 on negotiations, the documents used in venture capital funding are the letter of intent or term sheet, and the shareholders' agreement. The term sheet should contain the structure of the deal and a summary of key clauses.

The key clauses in the term sheet for venture capitalists, besides the usual warranties and covenants, are:

- key man insurance;
- right of co-sale if the entrepreneur obtains a buyer for all or some of his or her stock;
- pre-emptive right of first refusal on the issue of any new shares;
- agreed exit mechanism;
- board seat and right to monthly reports and cash flows; and
- remedies in the event of non-compliance and impending liquidation.

There are some other clauses that are matters of debate. One important issue is employee contracts. Experience has shown that employee contracts favour employees and seldom benefit the company. Many venture capitalists would recommend against signing service agreements. A service contract is useful if the buyer of a company wants the previous owner to stay around and run the company for one to two years while the buyer learns about the business. Often, however, the training period is shortened, by mutual consent.

Another important topic is the issue of guarantees. One description of a guarantor is a fool with a pen in his hand. While the many people regard the secret of venture capital as picking winners, the essence is more one of limiting losses. Venture capitalists should be prepared to lose all the capital they have invested in a company. They should not be required to lose more. It is better to put up the whole amount of risk capital as equity. Similarly, entrepreneurs often request a debt/equity mix. Venture capitalists should regard all the funds they provide as risk money. Debt funding should be provided by other parties. If venture capitalists must provide debt, it should be as convertible notes or have call options attached.

Anti-dilution provisions are another common subject of negotiation. These prevent the dilution of a shareholder's stake even if further funding is required. Investors should avoid these like the plague, especially if they are to be granted to an entrepreneur. In venture capital deals, where there will be several rounds of funding, seed investors should remember that such clauses will be a big negative to future investors because they cause the dilution effect to fall on the remaining parties. Future investors would have to seriously doubt the business acumen of any individual who would agree to such a clause. Moreover, because future investors will demand a similar clause, not only is it a special slice of the pie that cannot shrink; over time the slice begins to expand!

A clause most investors should consider including in a shareholders' agreement is the Mexican standoff, or call/put clause, especially when there are few parties with roughly equal ownership. Investors may be given the right to buy out the other parties. However, under a Mexican standoff, the other parties have the right to turn around and buy the offerer's interest at the same price. As the parties may not have similar wealth, often a long offer period is imposed (about six to nine months) to allow the less wealthy party to raise finance. The reason this clause is useful is that it keeps all parties honest. Entrepreneurs who are close to a business may realise the company is going to suddenly increase in value. They may try to buy out their present investors, conveniently forgetting the importance of their original contribution. Such a clause in the shareholders' agreement will always make one party stop and think before offering too low a value.

Finally, investors in a private company transaction must never allow themselves to be hurried. It is all too easy to buy; it is far harder to sell. When negotiating the shareholders' agreement it is worth remembering that whoever controls the documentation is in the more powerful position. Everyone says a contract once signed should go into the drawer and only be pulled out if something goes wrong. The investor should remind himself that Murphy was a venture capitalist. Something *will* go wrong and the agreements, articles of association and other documents will appear. Investors need to ensure, and here lawyers are essential, that their interests are protected if something goes amiss. No investor should ever hand over a cheque unless he or she has cosigned a shareholders' agreement with the entrepreneur, which both the investor's lawyers and the investor have agreed is a satisfactory protection of the investor's interests.

20 Post-investment activities

Lead venture capitalists usually take a board seat upon completion of the investment. The contribution of venture capitalists may be overstated, usually by venture capitalists themselves, especially when they make a successful investment. The Greeks best summarised the attitude when they said, 'Victory has many fathers but defeat is an orphan.'

In 1987 the Bureau of Industry Economics carried out an extensive survey of venture capitalists in Australia. Thirty-one venture capitalists said they provided management support as illustrated in Table 20.1.

The emphasis on financial management is not surprising, given that venture capitalists are essentially financial intermediaries. Venture capital is high-risk capital, typically in the form of equity, directed towards high rates of return. Venture capitalists invest in the future earnings potential of a business with little security and seek their return in the form of capital gain rather than through dividends.

The management of the businesses in which they invest usually have limited financial skills; venture capitalists provide a level of experience that previously was only available to clients of merchant banks and stock brokers. Indeed, it is the combination of entrepreneurs' business skills and venture capitalists' financial skills that provides much of the added value.

Whether board representation is a management support activity or a perk of the job is arguable. It has been my experience that when a board seat is offered in a high-growth company which has had a significant injection of equity, the queue of people willing to make the noble sacrifice of serving as a director is longer than one might expect.

Although most Australian venture capitalists see themselves as excellent general managers and astute marketers, nothing

Table 20.1 **Venture capitalists' management support**

Management support activity	% providing this activity
Financial management	71
Board representation	52
Marketing advice	45
Strategic advice	45
Product development	23
Recruiting	16

could be further from the truth. Proof of their general lack of marketing competence was amply demonstrated in the first year's fund-raising of the MICs in 1984 when, armed with a 100 per cent tax deduction, the first seven MICs could only raise $32.7 million of the $50 million allocated.

One of the better definitions of the venture capitalist's role was in Peter Drucker's stimulating book *Entrepreneurship and Innovation*. He defined the three key elements supplied by venture capitalists as follows:

* focus on the strategic plan;
* focus on the people; and
* focus on the financial needs of the company.

Focus on strategic plan

Businesses succeed on the whole not because the executives come up with the perfect plan, but because they decide on one course of action based on sound commercial principles. Management then executes the plan without distracting itself with outside activities.

McKinsey and Co. are probably the world's most reputable strategic management consultants. They deal regularly with the chief executives of the largest private and public organisations. The principal of a McKinsey office was once asked for the secret of its success. He replied that it was a matter of first establishing with the chief executive of the client organisation what were the three most important tasks for the next twelve months. The second step was to convince the chief executive not to spend any time on anything else. The final step was to reinforce the advice by charging a fee of $100 000 plus.

Entrepreneurs as a general rule are energetic people and

easily distracted. Venture capitalists need to ensure that a strategic plan is formally produced every year. It need not be a long document. Nevertheless, the exercise of defining what business you are in, applying the SWOT test (strengths, weaknesses, opportunities and threats) to the company, redefining the mission statement if necessary, and then setting just three corporate objectives for the following twelve months may perhaps be the most useful task a venture capitalist can perform for a business.

Strategic plans should be formulated every year as part of the budgeting process and after face-to-face contact with the more important customers. The role of venture capitalists is to ensure this task is done and then followed through. The Romans used to place a slave behind a successful general as he was riding on a chariot through the city in a triumphal procession. The slave would continually whisper in the ear of the general, 'Remember you are a mortal.' In the same way, venture capitalists should repeatedly be whispering in the ear of the entrepreneur, 'Remember the strategic plan—are you increasing the return to yourself and your shareholders?'

A big advantage of personal computers is that they make it very easy to update the plan of last year. Many entrepreneurs fail to realise that the fund-raising never stops. The secret is to put the fund-raising on a systematic rather than an ad hoc basis. A fundamental tool for success is an up-to-date formal business plan on the word processor. One of the most successful fund-raisers I know has the technique refined exquisitely. He only accepts equity injections in $500 000 – $750 000 tranches and each new tranche must be at a share price 50 per cent higher than the last. When approached by an investor, he produces a new plan from the word processor with the appropriate figures updated.

Where venture capitalists can be of significant help is in acting as a devil's advocate about the business plan. Active venture capitalists probably see three or four business plans a week. After a time they develop a feel for the likelihood of success. In this way they compensate for a weakness of smaller organisations — the lack of management depth. Large organisations have the management resources available to examine potential concepts thoroughly before making a decision. Weaknesses are rooted out and usually non-viable concepts are rejected. Major failures rarely occur; their scarcity accounts for the publicity received when they do.

Focus on the people

One golden rule of venture capital is that, given the choice between an 'A' class product with 'B' class people, or a 'B' class product with 'A' class people, one should choose the latter. In the BIE survey mentioned previously, the most common reason for rejection of business plans was inadequate management. Thus it is unusual to see recruitment ranked so low as a management support activity.

Drucker makes focusing on people a key task for venture capitalists. Much of the venture capitalist's job consists of meetings and interviews with a variety of people. They can act either as a screener or as a second opinion before hiring of key staff.

It is a principle of high-growth companies that they should over-hire. Over-hiring means the companies must recruit people who can handle more complex and sophisticated roles in three to four years time. Most important of all, the five key positions in the company, namely the general manager, the chief marketing officer, the chief financial officer, the chief operations/technical officer, and the chief legal officer, must be filled with able executives. The best executives are those who have had profit-centre experience with a division of a multinational company.

Small start-up companies often lack status. A venture capitalist with a high profile can be helpful in supplying credibility for such a small company. An established name serves to reassure both the recruiting agents and potential recruits. Entrepreneurs should remember it is not how much money is invested but who is investing that is often more important.

Focus on the financial needs of the company

Here venture capitalists can be of particular value in ensuring proper monthly accounting records are kept, annual budgets are prepared, and assisting in further rounds of funding.

Besides the actual investment made, venture capitalists must help the company source extra funds and lines of credit. Venture capitalists must dedicate some time in dealing with the bankers of the company. They should be able to arrange debt financing to act as bridging between rounds of equity. Venture capitalists can also help with the public listing. The procedures of under-writing, choosing a broker, preparing a prospectus and carrying out ASC and Stock Exchange negotiations are unfamiliar to entrepreneurs and typically only done once, while venture capitalists generally have experience of several listings.

One of the keys to the game is understanding that the company, if successful and growing, will need funds continu-ously and that these should be raised by successive rounds of equity. In Silicon Valley the companies have this process down to an art form and the chief financial officer, as soon as he or she has raised one round, immediately starts organising the next. Funds are traditionally raised on an annual basis.

The intelligent entrepreneur uses the annual fund-raising process to maintain control by playing a game of divide and conquer among the investors. A famous exponent is Jimmy Treybig of Tandem Computers. In 1985 I spent two weeks in the US visiting a number of successful venture capitalists. I could not understand how about ten of the funds all had 3 per cent of Tandem. What had happened was that the early venture capitalists who had taken, say, 15 per cent, had been diluted by later raisings and the last purchasers had been able to buy only 2–3 per cent of the company.

Entrepreneurs will often ask the initial venture capitalist to make a follow-on investment. The question often becomes one of either injecting new funds or pulling the plug. As a rule, if venture capitalists cannot attract a new party to co-invest in the next round, they themselves should not invest. This is another example of how syndication acts as an independent means of setting a valuation.

Besides raising cash, venture capitalists can also be of help in saving cash. It is fundamental to the success of a company that a culture of conserving cash prevails. One maxim is to 'lease the pencils'. Six-monthly cash forecasts must be prepared every month, and debtors and stock watched closely. Venture capital-ists should take an active role in preparing of cash forecasts, and in asset and liability management.

The other key financial role of venture capitalists is in introducing ratio analysis. 'Sell more' and 'Keep costs down' are useless statements. Aiming at $200 000 sales an employee and keeping overheads below 20 per cent of turnover, just as your competitors do, are measurable objectives.

Good venture capitalists should practise what they preach and prepare a monthly monitoring sheet, as shown in Appendix B. This is a simple spreadsheet which shows monthly actuals for income, balance-sheet items and cash flow and budgets. A number of key ratios are also calculated, along with the monthly breakeven point. Using a spreadsheet makes this an easy task. Moreover, if the package has a graphics capability it is easy to produce graphs for demonstrations at board meetings.

Venture capitalists perform several other functions. The legal protection of intellectual property is a difficult area, unfamiliar to many lawyers and often overlooked by small business. Licensing agreements, patents, trademarks and so on are expensive to arrange and venture capitalists could help save on legal costs and prevent costly mistakes. A key task is ensuring that all consultants who act for the company sign consulting agreements which pass to the company title for all inventions and designs made while employed by the company. Venture capitalists can also provide support in sales presentations to key suppliers and clients. However, if they can fulfil the role of emphasising the plan, the people and the finance, their contribution to the success of a business will be both significant and satisfying.

21 Exit mechanisms

Ultimately venture capital investors must look to exit from their investment. In this chapter we examine in detail two possible exit mechanisms: public listing and selling out to a third party. We assume the investor has built into the shareholders' agreement and share structure the third exit mechanism, which is redemption of original capital.

As indicated in Chapter 19, although at the beginning both parties may have sought public listing as an objective, the company may not grow to the size expected because the market is not of the size projected. The company will now join what venture capitalists call 'the living dead'. Suppose that after five years the company is producing $300 000 a year in after-tax profits and that venture capitalists had earlier bought one-third for $1 million. They would be looking at a yield of 10 per cent and the entrepreneur would be looking at a $200 000 tax-free income. While this is a reasonable return it is inadequate to cover other losses in the venture capital portfolio. The investors are locked in with nowhere to go. If, however, the investors have put into the shareholders' agreement a no dividend policy and forced redemption of investors' capital, they at least can get their capital back and go play the game somewhere else.

Public listing

In this section we shall examine the ways a company can go public. There are effectively three methods: the public offering, the compliance listing, and the backdoor listing. We will not try to describe them all in detail but will point out some of the key decisions. What is important, however, are the changes introduced by the new Corporations Law on 1 January 1991. Before that date, fund-raising by public offering required the registration and pre-vetting of a prospectus by the Corporate Affairs

Commission. Promoters would find their documents disappearing into a 'black hole' for ten to twenty weeks and then being asked a series of what appeared to be irrelevant questions. The whole emphasis on prospectuses has now changed. Promoters now have to prepare and register a prospectus with the Australian Securities Commission (ASC) which in turn must register it in 14 days or reject it for non-compliance. Instead of a long checklist of items a prospectus must contain all information that investors and their professional advisers reasonably require and reasonably expect to find in a prospectus for the purpose of making an informed assessment of assets and liabilities; financial position; profits and losses; prospects; and rights attaching to the securities.

If the prospectus is found to contain errors or misrepresentations, the promoters face both criminal and civil liabilities which are quite severe. The net of liability not only includes the company and directors but also those entities which previously could exclude themselves, such as promoters, stock brokers, underwriters, auditors, bankers, solicitors, and professional advisers and experts. The idea is that these individuals will now pre-vet the prospectus and the ASC registration should just be a rubber stamp. Indeed, there is a proposal to reduce the ASC vetting period from 14 to 2 days.

Public offering

One of the more unpleasant aspects of capitalism has been the history of wheeler-dealers raising funds from the public for various projects. The net result has been to convert the capital of the investors into income for the wheeler-dealers. The regulatory authorities in most countries have introduced laws to ensure that public offerings of shares are accompanied by a document known as a prospectus. This document should contain sufficient adequate and reliable information so the investor can judge the present financial condition of the company and its potential.

People involved in preparing a prospectus have duties of disclosure and of care. As stated previously, there have been significant changes in the law since the introduction of the Corporations Law on 1 January 1991. In addition, further changes are being mooted for the advertising and publicity which may take place at the time of the offer. While the changes at first received some negative publicity about costs, most of it was due to lack of familiarity with the new rules. It is noticeable that since the new rules were introduced in January 1991 the legal, accounting and advisory costs expressed as a percentage of funds raised have shown a steady decline from over 1 per cent to less than a quarter of a per cent. On the other hand, there are significant benefits under the system in the reduction of time taken, quality and content of prospectuses.

Furthermore, the Australian Stock Exchange (ASX) has its own listing rules and regulations. These are the rules covering the number of shareholders, profit history, types of shares allowed and so on. They also changed significantly on 1 January 1992. The minimum spread of shareholders is 500 persons and each must be holding a share parcel to the value of at least $2000. This imposes a minimum capitalisation of $1 000 000 on the company. The company must have had a pre-income-tax aggregated operating profit of at least $1 000 000 over the past three full financial years. It must have had unqualified audited accounts for the past three full financial years. It must have been in the same predominant business activity for a minimum of three full financial years. Finally the company must have had a pre-income-tax operating profit of at least $400 000 for the twelve months prior to the lodging of a prospectus. These are exactly the types of companies the venture capitalists and entrepreneurs should be trying to build.

On the other hand, it may comfort those about to start the Initial Public Offering (IPO) route to remember that others have trod the path before. Over 350 companies listed on the ASX main board in the three year period 1984–87. The stock market, even discounting the October 1987 crash, showed explosive growth during the 1980s. Australian equity turnover as a percentage of gross domestic product has increased from 4 per cent in 1983 to 17 per cent in 1991. While there was a collapse in confidence and a flight to liquidity in 1989–91 there has been a recent resurgence in new float activity. In the last six months of 1991 $1.9 billion was raised compared with $3 million in the previous six.

As has been stated several times, the goal of both the entrepreneur and venture capitalists is a public listing to achieve the greatest capital gain. Consequently the company should have already appointed reputable auditors and solicitors. The first critical step after deciding to float the company is to appoint an underwriter.

Underwriters guarantee that the funds required will be raised at a specific time and under specific terms. The underwriter must take up the balance, referred to as the shortfall, of any amount sought and not raised. Appointing an underwriter is most important, and should not be left to chance or personal contact. As in most purchase decisions, the buyer should contact at least three underwriters and ask why the company should choose one over the others.

The first criterion of choice is the after-market support the underwriter can provide. Listing is not just a means of raising money or profile. It also provides negotiability for stock. If the underwriter cannot convince the entrepreneur that it will provide after-market support by promoting the company to the investing institutions and private clients, the entrepreneur should look elsewhere. Therefore it is probably better to ensure that the underwriter is a stockbroker or a stockbroker is intimately involved. To measure the after-market support, ask the underwriter to provide the price and volume history graphs since listing of the last three stocks it has underwritten. The underwriter should price the issue at 15–20 per cent under the expected market price to ensure after-market support. These profits are known as 'stag' profits, in contrast to the bulls and bears of the stock market. If the price falls after the issue, one may assume the underwriter has lost credibility in the market.

Besides the price–volume graphs, the company should ask to see the latest three prospectuses and ask which institutions subscribed to the issues. This will provide some measure of how the market views the underwriter. The stockbroking industry has fairly high staff turnover and institutions tend to follow individuals.

It is also necessary to establish which representative of the underwriter is going to be advising on the issue and what is his experience. IPOs are not difficult, as the listing figures above attest, but there are some horror stories of companies failing to list on schedule owing to oversight caused by lack of experience and thousands of copies of prospectuses being shredded.

Another criterion is the financial capacity of the underwriter and its ability to meet a shortfall. In times of boom, capital strength is overlooked, but when there is a correction it becomes important. It is necessary to understand that underwriting is risky business. While the fees appear high compared to the work done, every so often an issue takes a bath and the shortfall is large. The cash flow in underwriting consists of a stream of reasonable profits interspersed with the occasional large loss. All underwriters understand this problem; they try to delay signing the underwriting agreement as long as possible and insert as many escape clauses as they can. On the other hand, if there is a market correction but the expected shortfall is a small part of its capital base, it is likely the underwriter will still go ahead. If, however, the shortfall is a large part of its capital base then the underwriter will pull out of the agreement. The company has limited redress; suing an underwriter will not gain the support it will ultimately want from the financial community.

Finally, the company should try to establish the fee structure and terms of the issue. Typical fees including brokerage range from 3 per cent to 5 per cent but they can go higher for speculative issues.

Once the underwriter has been chosen, work can commence. The underwriter should immediately prepare a timetable and a list of the parties involved. The new rules mean that with focused effort an IPO can take about three months. The company must appoint an executive responsible for the various documents and the roadshow presentation. This is usually the financial director or the company secretary. The company will need to draft the marketing part of the prospectus. It will need to ensure that the necessary board resolutions and shareholders' meetings occur. The investigating accountants must complete their report on time. As a full audit must be completed no more than six months before listing, many companies list in the third quarter of the calendar year following the June 30 close. The company should appoint someone to maintain the share register. Finally the responsible executive must organise the preparation for the roadshow. This refers to the visits to and by institutional investors and major private clients at the time of selling the issue, which is after registration of the prospectus and before listing.

A key IPO decision is the pricing and structure of the issue. Each IPO is different—but regulations forbid the raising of further equity funds at less than the par value of the share. Hence if a company has the choice of issuing shares at par value of 50c or at a 20c premium on a 30c par, it should choose the latter. Markets can change and the need to raise funds may coincide with the bottom of a market cycle. It is prudent to build in a premium if possible.

Because an IPO is new, exciting and technically fascinating, many companies fail to use it as a marketing weapon. The prospectus can be a most useful sales aid, yet it is surprising how many prospectuses fail to contain such simple details as the locations and telephone numbers of the company's branch offices. Moreover, the executives should make sure they reserve sufficient shares for distribution to clients and suppliers. Stock brokers do not just do underwritings for the fee income. If the company is successful and a broker becomes known as the broker for the stock it will earn far more in commissions. Even more important, if it can provide stag profits for its clients it will generate loyalty for new deals. Newly listed companies should also use the loyalty created by stag profits by placing shares among their clients, employees, and suppliers.

Compliance listing

Before the introduction of the new regulations in January 1991 the big problem with the prospectus route was time, usually a minimum of six months and more often nine months. To speed up the process other techniques evolved, of which the most popular was private placement combined with a non-renounceable rights issue. This was known as a 'compliance' listing as the issue complied with the Australian Stock Exchange listing requirements. Using this method the company did not need to prepare and register a prospectus. This has now changed. A prospectus is necessary under the new rules so the compliance method is effectively 'dead'.

Back-door listings

One of the benefits of capitalism is that failed companies eventually lose their value and their resources are allocated elsewhere. On every stock exchange there are listed companies which have lost their original means of producing profits and have slowly lost all value. What remains is a shell. The present shareholders have their scrip at the bottom of a drawer or on the wall. Listing by the back door consists first of buying up to

19.9 per cent of the shell in order not to breach the takeover provisions of the Corporations Code. A shareholders' meeting is held to allow a consolidation of capital of the shell company so that the net tangible assets per share will be roughly equal to the par value of the share. On completion of the consolidation, the shell company then issues as consideration a sufficient number of new shares in exchange for all the shares of the target company. The new issue requires majority approval of the shareholders other than the acquirer and his associates. Usually the incumbent shareholders are so happy to see something positive finally happening to the company that they approve the resolutions with alacrity. To ensure the consideration is fair and reasonable the authorities require an independent expert's valuation of the acquired company.

A back-door listing is a form of reverse takeover in which a smaller company by issuing shares takes over a larger company. Typical shells have a market capitalisation of $300 000 or less and the acquired companies will be valued at $5 million upwards.

The IPO is the king hit in venture capital. The current Australian financial environment favours the IPO as an exit more than does the US. Not only is the exit price lower (US companies typically require a $US2 million earnings figure to obtain institutional support) but the escrow provisions in Australia are less stringent. In Australia pre-IPO shareholders typically have their shares held in escrow for a year. In the US they may only dribble to the market 1 per cent of their holding every quarter.

The problem with public listings is timing. The market for new issues is cyclical and the window is not always open for new listings. The bull market in the 1980s caused the number of listed companies on the ASX Main Board to rise steeply, but in the four years post 1987, new issues were infrequent and the total numbers gradually declined by 30 per cent.

Selling out to a third party

The other alternative to the IPO is selling out to a third party. Surveys in the US show that acquisitions occur three times more often than IPOs. Large companies, particularly those with mature products and steady cash flows, prefer to buy profitable companies rather than build up businesses from nothing. A mature listed company in order to maintain its stock price must show steady growth in earnings. Starting new entities is expensive, especially if the management uses equity to fund the start-up. On the other hand, buying an already operating and profitable company entails less risk. Moreover, the purchase can increase earnings per share if it is done by debt and if the pre-tax profit of the business is greater than the interest costs. Even if the purchase is financed with shares, provided the P/E of the purchase is less than the P/E of the acquiring company, then the earnings per share of the acquiring company will increase.

The other acquisition method becoming increasingly common is the leveraged buy-out. While fast-growth companies are not typically LBO targets, if the business growth has topped and expected growth is declining, then the company may well be a candidate.

An active and bullish stock market will tend to increase both merger activity and acquisition prices. Timing the merger of a company is as important as timing an IPO.

The private company should try to create a market by talking to more than one buyer. Far too often a business accepts the first offer. By creating a market, the shareholders will have a better chance of obtaining a fair and reasonable price.

It is probably best to use an intermediary. Selling a business is similar to selling a house. Real estate agents would rather get a smaller fee on a fire sale than no fee at all. A good method of obtaining fair value is to ladder the fee. For example, if you think your company is worth $10 million, say you will pay the agent 0.5 per cent for the first $10 million, 3 per cent for the next $5 million and 30 per cent for any amounts received over $15 million. Using a laddered fee can do wonders for the 'independent valuation' your expert will provide when you begin negotiations.

Brokers have a difficult problem because they earn by pure commission and such deals can take nine months to consummate. Many brokers will ask for an up-front fee; a laddered fee should enable entrepreneurs to persuade brokers that they should receive commissions only for success.

Another tactic is to make sure the profits are as high as possible. If the company has been supporting a loss-making branch it should close the branch. Accounts should be audited and physical stocktakes done regularly. Surplus cash should not be left in the company. The company should take out options on renewing any leases. Many businesses lose much of their value if their lease is about to run out and is not renewable.

A problem with a company sale is confidentiality. If information about a potential sale leaks out, employees and customers may begin to get nervous and competitors may start spreading rumours about the financial stability of the company.

Just as the venture capital investor is aware that the structure of the deal is as important as the valuation, so when selling a company the terms may be more important than the price.

A key determinant in any sale is the effect of tax. Tax considerations usually determine whether the sale consists of assets or shares. Because stamp duty is so much lower for shares (0.6 per cent) than assets (as high as 5.5 per cent) it is more common to sell shares. In consideration the sellers generally want cash, although venture capital companies may be more comfortable with shares. Often consideration can be a mixture of shares and cash and the vendors may receive different proportions.

One benefit often proposed for asset sales is that the acquiring company does not take over the liabilities of the acquisition. While this is true, an asset acquirer will still need to negotiate with clients, suppliers and employees. Often clauses are inserted in distribution and maintenance agreements which allow termination if there is a change of ownership, but these are rarely enforced.

A typical request by purchasers, especially if the deal is a leveraged buy-out, is some form of vendor finance, typically a promissory note. A seller's note may be structured in a number of ways. The bank will want delayed payment of principal and the purchaser will want a low rate of interest. However, a seller's note may be the concession that makes or breaks a sale. One difficulty with deferred payments is capital gains tax, which states that all payments are deemed immediately payable and that full capital gain arises immediately on disposal of the asset.

If the sale is an asset sale, and there are some pre-September 1985 assets and vendor finance is required, one approach is to agree to purchase the assets later at a higher price, reflecting the current rate of interest. In that way the seller will not have to pay any income tax on interest received. Although the purchaser will not obtain any deduction for interest, he will achieve a higher cost-base for the asset and a potential capital gains tax saving.

Another problem with share sales and vendor finance is the prohibition in the Corporations Law against companies providing financial assistance for acquiring their own shares except in specific circumstances. However, the shareholders by special resolution at a general meeting can authorise such assistance, provided it is advertised in the daily newspapers. If neither members, creditors, nor the Australian Securities Commission object, the vendor finance may proceed 21 days after publication.

Another common request is for the entrepreneur to stay with the company for several years and the purchase price to be adjusted according to either future earnings or revenue. While profit is the usual criterion, both parties may find it preferable to agree on revenue as a basis for valuation. But if profit is the basis, it is common for the seller to reduce all forms of long-term expenditure, be it capital equipment, product or market development, replacement stock and so on. Sellers may shelter some of the purchase price by taking some of the payment as a consulting agreement. While capital gain is indexed against inflation, salaries are taxed initially at a lower rate and the entrepreneur will also be able to shelter some salary with superannuation.

Entrepreneurs should also develop an understanding of how prospective acquirers operate. Many entrepreneurs have ended up staying with and eventually running the acquiring company. In fact if the entrepreneur sees such an opportunity, he might well accept either a lower price or a consideration containing a larger amount of the acquirer's stock.

Because most sales will be of shares rather than assets, representations and warranties will be needed from both the entrepreneur and the venture capitalist. Here venture capitalists, with experience on the other side of the table, should ensure fair and reasonable terms for all parties. Also, purchase agreements will usually contain some form of non-compete agreement based on some mixture of location, product, and time. While the non-compete domain can be set quite wide, it will be difficult to uphold in court.

Both stock and asset sales are complicated transactions, due to the tax implications. The past decade has seen changes in company tax every year and many areas of the tax code require rulings from the authorities. Also the laws will change over time, so all parties need professional advice. One reason for using a big auditing firm is that it should have expert tax partners. Another is the possibility of the fourth exit mechanism, receivership. This is not the book in which to consider winding up and liquidations. However, investors should realise that entrepreneurs tend to be optimistic till the removal of the telephones. Thus the investors must provide the realism. The earlier realism sets in, the more likely it is that investors will be able to recover some of their investment. Also, the investors should ensure they participate in any sale discussions. Often entrepreneurs wishing to save their own skins and gain credibility with new buyers will forget their fiduciary duties to present shareholders. They will team up with the new buyers and try to persuade the current investors to accept a fire-sale valuation. It is galling to decline what turns out to be a good investment opportunity. But it does not compare with what investors on the wrong side of a fire sale feel when they suddenly see their disposal become a successful business.

PART V

MANAGING A VENTURE CAPITAL FUND

22 Fund formation and structures

The final part of this book addresses the organisation or individual who invests in more than one venture capital investment and is effectively managing a venture capital portfolio. It comprises three chapters. This chapter examines the formation and organisation of a venture capital fund, Chapter 23 analyses operations, and the final chapter discusses portfolio management.

While amateur entrepreneurs complain about the lack of venture capital in Australia, there is probably more of a surplus. The problem is in the definition. There has never been and probably never will be sufficient money available to fund the development of production prototypes of all the inventions developed in Australia. There is a surplus of money to invest in high-growth companies which have the potential to expand. The mistake is to think that venture capital is start-up and seed capital. Even in the US it comprises only a small part of the venture capitalist's portfolio. In April 1988 the accounting firm Ernst & Whinney published what was probably the first detailed and comprehensive survey of venture capital organisations in Australia. The survey showed that besides the eleven MICs there were at least fourteen government organisations and over 60 private sector enterprises dedicated solely or in part to providing venture capital. While many of these have disappeared there is still a surplus of development capital.

The more important word in the phrase 'venture capital' is capital. Unfortunately far too many investors imitate the entrepreneurs in whom they invest and become overly intrigued by the venture side of the business.

In the US the typical venture capital fund structure is a limited partnership. In a standard partnership the partners are liable on a joint and several basis. If one partner fails to meet his share of the partnership debts, creditors and lenders may look to other partners for settlement on either a joint or individual basis. In a limited partnership the limited partners can only lose all of their original investment. A general partner, who may be one individual or more, manages the partnership for an annual fee and a share in the generated capital gains. The partnership agreement often precludes the general partner from starting another fund until the achievement of certain gains. The agreement also includes restrictions such as those put on company directors to ensure duties of faith and care and prevent conflicts of interest. The fund usually has a termination date within seven to ten years with an option to extend the partnership annually. Investors prefer the limited partnership structure not only because early losses can be offset against income for tax, but because it is easy to dissolve and distribute the spoils, which should comprise a mixture of cash and shares in listed companies and not incur either capital transfer or capital gains taxes. Limited partnerships have only recently become legal in most Australian states and are so severely restricted that their utility as a financial structure is untested. The change in the August 1992 Budget where the taxation treatment of a limited partnership is to be the same as a company means it is unlikely they will be used widely.

Moreover, now that public trading trusts are subject to corporate tax (with the proviso that all income distributions are franked and so escape further taxation), the preferred structure for the Australian venture capital fund (VCF) is the limited liability company. Several of the venture capital funds have a separate management company to manage the venture capital fund for a set fee. The management company has an equity incentive in the form of either options or partly paid shares. One advantage of the management company structure is the comfort provided to investors of an upper limit on management costs. Unfortunately, if there is no limit self-interest may lead to imprudent charges and inadequate funds may be available for investment.

Some people think venture capitalists are motivated by capital gain and that the management fee is only to cover operating costs. On the other hand, it is worth comparing the income generated by the management fee to the capital gain payout. The capital gain kicker typically varies from 15 to 25 per cent. As Table 22.1 shows, a fund which has a management fee of 4 per cent and a 20 per cent capital gain incentive obtains

Table 22.1   Equity kickers versus management fees

Year	Fund size	Equity kicker	4%	Management fee cumulative
1	10	0.00	0.40	0.40
2	10	0.00	0.40	0.80
3	10	0.00	0.40	1.20
4	12.9	0.58	0.52	1.72
5	16.7	1.33	0.67	2.38
6	21.5	2.30	0.86	3.24
7	27.8	3.55	1.11	4.35
8	35.8	5.17	1.43	5.78

Note: Expected average growth 20% compound per year at end of eight years. Fund stays the same size for first three years then grows at rate to give 20% compound growth. The table shows the value of the equity incentive if the fund is closed earlier and the cumulative management fees earned by termination.

more income from the management fee over the life of the fund than from the equity kicker. This is because the management agreements for nearly all types of funds specify that the fee is a percentage of the higher issued capital or net assets.

The other protection usually introduced by the managers is some form of golden share arrangement. A golden share ensures that a vote of the investor shareholders may not remove the managers. It is a share that holds a controlling interest if a meeting tables certain types of shareholders' resolutions.

The other important component of the financial structure is the underwriting fee to ensure the raising of funds. Fund-raising in Australia appears to need a minimum underwriting fee of 4 per cent and there will be a need for additional incentives for the underwriters in the form of higher fees or options if the product is to attract funds from retail investors.

We shall now review the financial structures of some of the venture capital firms in Australia, as they provide a practical guide.

Austech Ventures Limited

Austech was one of the first MICs. It is now managed by the Melbourne-based Investment Management Australia group. The original management was a separate entity and was to receive a fee of $150 000 plus 2.4 per cent of funds under management. On the original fund size of $7 million the income equation

represented a fee of 4.5 per cent. The equity kicker was provided by 1000 'M' class redeemable preference shares owned
by the management, which entitled the holder to 20 per cent
of any capital increase. The management could only be changed
with the approval of the 'M' class shareholders. The management was further protected by the inability of the company to
redeem the shares for four years after the date of issue. The
Austech issue was not underwritten and the proposed brokerage
was 2 per cent. The MIC Licensing Board annual reports indicate
that Austech failed to gain much investor support during the
first MIC fund-raising efforts of June 1984. The last week in June
(which is the last week of the Australian fiscal year) is the
traditional time when most Australian tax-shelter funds raise
money.

Australian Innovation Limited

Australian Innovation Limited is the new name of the former
BT Innovation Limited (BTIL) which was another original MIC.
BTIL was managed by a separate entity for a fee of 4 per cent.
Options were issued on the basis of one share for every five
shares on issue (which is equivalent to an equity kicker of 16.7
per cent of the capital gain achieved) to provide the management incentive. The underwriting fee was 4 per cent and BTIL
was one of the few original MICs to be significantly oversub-
scribed.

Westintech Innovation Corporation Limited

Westintech was another original MIC which left the program in
November 1988 and, after focusing on aeronautical products,
was taken over by the Australian multinational TNT. The original
company was managed internally but the management and
directors only had 50 000 options, or a ride of 0.5 per cent. The
company was unusual in giving the original 70 subscribers a
1:1 option sweetener and a pre-emptive entitlement on a 1:1
basis for the first issue of $5 million. The underwriting fee was
effectively 4 per cent. The management protected its position
by a sliding scale of voting rights set up as follows:

- 1 vote for every 20 shares up to 400 shares;
- 1 vote for every 40 shares between 400 and 800;

- 1 vote for every 100 shares between 800 and 25 per cent of the company; and
- no votes for any shares above 25 per cent of the total issued.

Thus if an entity held 50.1 per cent of the 9.77 million shares on issue it would have 24 495 votes. The management, by ensuring that 1225 friends each purchased 400 shares or 5 per cent of the issued capital, could block a takeover.

Continental Venture Capital Limited

CVC was a second-round MIC which has proved to be very successful in terms of fund-raising. As of 30 June 1991 it had raised over $95 million. The company has internal management but the incentive is only one option for every ten shares on issue. The underwriting fee was 4.5 per cent.

CP Ventures Limited

CP Ventures was another second-round MIC which subsequently, after raising more capital than any other MIC, has given up its licence and is now managed by IMA. Originally it was managed by a separate management company for a fee of 3.5 per cent. The managers kept control with special managers' shares that had a par value of 1c compared to the ordinary shares with a par value of $1. The managers' shares were issued on a 1:4 basis and ranked on a par with ordinary shares for any distributions or if there was a capital gain. Only the holders of the managers' shares could vote on issues of appointment or dismissal of the manager. The underwriting fee was 5.3 per cent and the underwriters were also granted options for a further 4.2 per cent fully diluted equity in the company.

First MIC Limited & H-G Ventures Limited

The same management company, Hambro Grantham, for a fee of 3 per cent adjusted by the CPI each year, manages both of these venture capital companies. The manager holds all the sponsor ordinary shares, which have 50 per cent of the voting power in all resolutions about terminating management contracts. The sponsor ordinary shares are entitled to 20 per cent of all dividend and capital distributions.

Transequity Limited

Transequity was a Hobart second-board venture capital company which raised $7 million in the second half of 1986 by the issue of 14 million 25c shares at a premium of 25c. The subscribers obtained as a sweetener a free option on a 1:2 formula. The promoters issued themselves 9 million partly paid shares and 4.5 million options and had 1 million options available to issue to management as an incentive. The underwriters charged 4 per cent and were issued 700 000 options representing 2 per cent of the fully diluted capital. Since listing, Transequity has had a somewhat chequered history.

These examples are not definitive; the appropriate structure depends on market conditions, managers' track record, endorsements and so on. The required management track record will be discussed in the next chapter. For fund-raising, however, endorsement would be a critical issue. Australia 'rides on the sheep's back'. Australian investors tend to copy sheep and follow the endorsement of a major institution. One or two well-known lead investors are essential for raising the necessary funds.

Another type of venture capital fund is one which is either corporate or institution sponsored and operates as a subsidiary. Overseas the corporate venture capital funds have had limited success. One reason for failure has been the staff chosen to operate the funds. Engineers or corporate planners are usually chosen, and they make the common mistake of thinking (possibly correctly) that if they were running the business it would be a success. The policies of the parent corporation towards remuneration and personnel development will often conflict with those needed for venture capital funds. The parent corporation's policies will be based on salaries and probably incorporate job rotation every two to three years. A venture capital manager is motivated by capital gains, which needs a longer-term perspective. Another difficulty for a corporate VCF is that the capital investment process adopted is similar to that used for capital equipment. Capital investments are carefully considered and subject to the overall capital budget of the corporation, which can vary quarter by quarter. Finally, corporations tend to demand control and are uncomfortable either in syndications or in taking new partners for further fund-raisings.

The next question is the fund-raising target. A minimum of

$10 million is necessary. A smaller total amount does not allow sufficient portfolio diversification if a fund has a reasonable minimum investment level. Otherwise adequate diversification is only achieved with insufficiently sized investments. Too much money can be raised. While megafunds (funds larger than $100 million) are unusual in Australia they have become common in the US. Their performance has been mediocre.

First there is a tendency to put too much cash into a deal trying to lay off funds. As the failure of Impact Systems demonstrated, too much equity funding can do as much harm as too little.

Second, the megafunds do not syndicate; they tend to do the entire deal themselves. Syndication is useful to venture capitalists, not so much because of risk diversification but because it provides a method of independently pricing and testing a deal. If several contemporaries refuse to invest for logical reasons, perhaps the deal should be reconsidered It is the same as an underwriter looking for sub-underwriters; if an underwriter cannot lay off some of the risk onto professional investors it will drop a proposed underwriting. A venture capital fund should use syndication as independent confirmation of a deal.

Finally, megafunds will have a tendency when coming up to a refinancing to throw money at an investment instead of refusing. Again, when refinancing or the next round is due, the earlier investors should look to having at least one new party in the round. If the original investors cannot induce a new party to join the deal, they must reconsider their position and ensure they are not throwing good money after bad. Thus too much money can be as much of a problem as too little. A good size for a venture capital fund is probably between $15 million and $25 million.

The final matter to be considered by a venture capital fund is location. Miller and Cote in their article 'Growing the Next Silicon Valley' surveyed the attempts of all the various governments, public and local authorities in the world to create Silicon Valleys. The article suggested that for a similar cluster to have a chance of surviving four factors were needed:

Universities in the forefront of technology which let out research contracts

Scientists are not entrepreneurs, they are passive suppliers of

technology. Most research in universities and government lab-
oratories is not market driven and rarely results in commercial
products or enterprises. Entrepreneurs, by contrast, are active
developers of technology. Yet this distinction is not understood
in Australia. Indeed the reverse philosophy holds sway with
many Australian universities looking for funds to internally
develop non-commercial products instead of offering funds and
people to outside organisations. Universities are generally poor
incubators of entrepreneurs and high-growth products.

While the universities so far have not become incubators, it
is pleasing to note the introduction of prototype funding contracts by the federal government. The Telecom Product Development Fund and the National Procurement Development
Program are excellent initiatives which, in the few years they
have been operating, have already generated a number of
commercially successful products.

A pool of venture capitalists

In the US venture capitalists act not only as a source of venture
capital but as screeners and developers of enterprises. Compared with large organisations where the management team has
depth, entrepreneurs at the beginning walk alone. Venture capitalists, who spend their time looking at business plans, meeting
entrepreneurs and monitoring businesses, develop knowledge
and skills to help entrepreneurs. Government efforts to supply
development capital either by generous grants or government
funds are usually self-defeating and prevent a pool of venture
capitalists forming. Successful investors must be trained by the
marketplace. Bureaucrats are poor marksmen and usually
poorer at picking winners. It is interesting to compare the
strategies of New South Wales and Victoria. In Victoria the
Victorian Economic Development Corporation (VEDC)
swamped the marketplace with soft loans and equity venture
capital offered at very high valuations. The VEDC ultimately
collapsed and was the subject of a searing report. In contrast
the aid given by the New South Wales Government has been
small. Yet the venture capital centre of Australia is Sydney, with
many more active venture capital participants. Slowly but surely
a pool of professional venture capitalists is developing in
Sydney.

Entrepreneurship is a virtue and not a vice

In the US the entrepreneurs have become cult-like figures. There the financial community and the media distinguish between the builders of businesses and wheeler-dealers. Unfortunately the same distinction was not made in Australia. The media attached the word entrepreneur to many wheeler-dealers. Indeed the Stock Exchange has developed a list of companies known as entrepreneurial investors which contains few if any true entrepreneurs. The classic definition is someone who shifts economic resources out of an area of lower and into an area of higher productivity and yield. In the US entrepreneurs are individuals who build up businesses from scratch by creating new products or processes which the market buys. Examples of individuals and companies which would fit into the US definition would be Sir Peter Abeles of TNT, Sir Tristan Antico of Pioneer Concrete, and Paul Trainor of Nucleus. Some of the examples quoted in the media, particularly the New Zealand 'entrepreneurs', were laughable. Building up a highly leveraged conglomerate with the occasional astute purchase is a well-known phenomenon which happens again and again during periods of easy credit such as occurred in Australia in the 1980s. The people who organise such entities are typically charismatic individuals who are good at turning other people's capital into their income. 'Wheeler-dealer' describes such individuals perfectly. In the bull market many of these individuals had well-publicised runs. Events after the October 1987 crash have displayed the relative strengths of these individuals and the corporations they built. Unfortunately the media focus has given 'entrepreneurship' a bad name. The wheeler-dealers began as one-man bands; they are finishing as one-man bands.

Minimum size of market

In the US another often-quoted necessity for developing a Silicon Valley are good physical amenities. Ocean, sunshine, low crime rates and so on are necessary requirements; all of the mainland state capital cities in Australia would be suitable candidates. However there is a minimum market size needed to adequately test most products and provide a catchment area with enough customers to fund the initial development of a business. Marketing experts in the US regard the US market as divided into 100 segments, the minimum market segment comprising 2 million people. Extending such logic to Australia means the best location of a venture capital fund is either Sydney or Melbourne.

However, the most important determinant for fund-raising success is the overall condition of the financial markets. Is the equity window open? The management track record then follows. While prospective venture capitalists can do little about the former, they can do something about the latter. The following chapter describes the management skills needed to operate a venture capital company.

23 How to run a venture capital fund

Before we describe how to run a VCF it is worth noting how a VCF resembles other forms of financial intermediaries, such as banks and building societies. First, a VCF seeks funds from a number of investors, which it in turn invests. Second, the VCF invests in many different enterprises to diversify risk. Third, the VCF by professional management and more efficient administration tries to achieve a higher return than investors who make their own direct investment into private companies.

Nevertheless, the investments of a VCF are different from those of other financial intermediaries. High-growth companies lack the performance history on which to judge the investment. The investment is illiquid for a considerable time. There is also the implicit recognition by the investor that the business will need more funds. Finally, the investment usually needs a much greater degree of hands-on involvement by the managers of the fund.

Little scientific research has been done on how to run a VCF. One US paper (by Tyebjee & Bruno) published the results of a telephone survey of 46 venture capitalists and a detailed analysis of 90 investments made by 41 different venture capitalists The Tyebjee & Bruno paper developed a model, shown schematically in Figure 23.1. A model VCF performs in a five-step process.

In this chapter we will compare the Tyebjee & Bruno model with information gained from the MIC Licensing Board annual reports and the Australia Venture Capital Survey and Report produced by Ernst & Whinney. The Ernst & Whinney survey was the result of a mail questionnaire to which 56 companies replied.

Step 1—deal origination

Tyebjee & Bruno analysed the origin of completed deals as follows:

- unsolicited cold calls   25 per cent
- referrals   65 per cent
- active search   10 per cent

The rate of referrals is due in part to the substantial syndication that occurs in the US. Syndication refers to the process whereby one VCF, acting as a lead investor, seeks other funds to participate. Syndication is a method of both diversifying risk and performing due diligence and valuation. The greatest comfort an investor can have is to know there is another investor making the same decision. Syndication is now becoming more common in Australia. For example as of 30 June 1987 the total number of MIC investments was 115 while the MICs themselves had made a total of 141 investments (indicating that a maximum of 26 deals, or 23 per cent, were syndicated among MICs). The figure for syndications is even higher, with a number of non-MIC funds now investing.

Figure 23.1 How a venture capital company operates

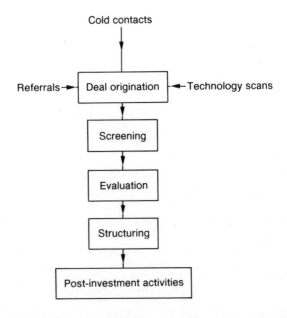

The other source of referrals is from entrepreneurs and the advisory network. Successful entrepreneurs who know the venture capital game are probably the best source of deals. Thus a golden circle of investment can begin where a budding entrepreneur either works for or asks the advice of successful entrepreneurs. If successful entrepreneurs detect the entrepreneurial spirit, they pass the carrier on to the venture capitalists and a new business success story may begin. Similarly, auditors and lawyers who work on successful deals develop reputations which further attract future successful entrepreneurs.

In Australia the networks are new and developing. However, the VCF fund should try to develop networks so the fund is the recipient of a deal flow. Some of these networks are already formed. Hambro Grantham has developed, for example, an alliance with the Commonwealth Trading Bank.

Another source of deal flow has been the Enterprise Workshops. An Enterprise Workshop is a year-long program in which budding entrepreneurs attend a group of seminars and week-long live-in courses, learn to analyse business plans and then prepare a business plan for a new venture. Some excellent venture capital investments, such as Dataplex and Vision Systems, started life in Enterprise Workshops.

Step 2—screening

A VCF tends to run on a small staff. Given a good deal flow, it is necessary to set up screening criteria to select proposals for further investigation. The Tyebjee & Bruno paper found that most VCFs used the following criteria:

- *Size of the investment and the policy of the venture fund:* An implicit lower limit is set on investment size because each investment takes around the same time to monitor and venture capitalists cannot afford to spread themselves too thin. The monitoring limit is five to eight investments per manager compared to, say, 30–40 equity investments for the average insurance or super fund portfolio manager who operates in a hands-off style. At the top end, there is a limit set by the size of the fund. No prudent fund manager would expose more than 10 per cent of his portfolio to one investment. The Tyebjee & Bruno study revealed a range of individual investment sizes from $30 000 to $7.5 million with

Figure 23.2 MIC investment profile 1988–89

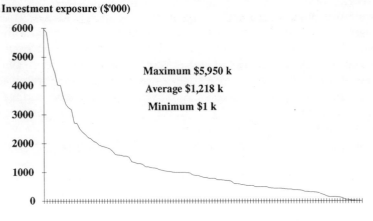

Investment exposure ($'000)

> Maximum $5,950 k
> Average $1,218 k
> Minimum $1 k

MIC Annual Report 1988-89 (117 investments)

the median size being $1 million. One-third of the deals were for more than $1.5 million and another third were for less than $500 000. In the US, syndication is the rule and over 80 per cent of the deals done involve more than one VCF. The MIC Licensing Board annual reports provide the first good sample of venture capital investment in Australia. The MIC investment profile for 1988–89, which is the largest sample available, is shown in Figure 23.2 and the cumulative investment graph in Figure 23.3. Investment exposure is the sum of equity investment, loans, and loan guarantees. The exposure varies from $6.1 million to $10 000. The mean investment exposure was $1 256 000 and the median investment exposure was $887 500, which are comparable to the US figures. Over 46 per cent of the investments were above $1 million while 27 per cent were below $500 000. Moreover, of these latter investments, sixteen were below $250 000. Disregarding these sixteen investments as aberrations born out of inexperience, the median investment would be $1 000 000. The investment profile in Australia appears to be similar to that in the US. The smaller number of syndications in Australia has probably led to the higher single exposures, and the lack of experience has probably meant that the venture capitalists in such cases were unable to walk away from a deal but continued in some cases to throw good money after bad.

Figure 23.3 MIC cumulative investment graph

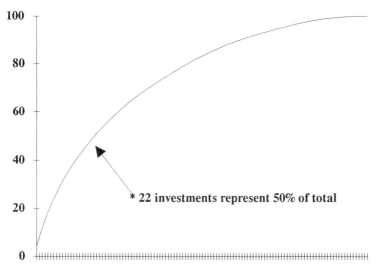

Cumulative %

MIC Annual Report 1988-89 (117 investments)

- *The technology and market sector of the venture* : This is the next most important criterion. In general venture capitalists are investing as much in an industry as in an individual business. They cannot hope to understand more than a few industries so implicit specialisation occurs. In general, venture capitalists prefer products to services, the industrial to the consumer market, and nascent to mature technology when investing in high-growth companies.
- *Geographic location of the venture* : Since venture capitalists should meet regularly with the key management, they prefer to choose nearby investments. Although VCFs usually state they will accept proposals from anywhere, over time their portfolios develop a geographic specialisation. This trend has already appeared in Australia even in the short time the MIC program has run. The location of the head office of an MIC has a substantial bearing on the choice of investment. Table 23.1 shows how the majority of businesses and investment funds are in the same state as the VCF head office.
- *Stage of financing*: Venture capital infusions occur at several stages during the life cycle of a venture. Table 23.2 shows

the amounts and numbers of businesses funded as recorded for 1986 by *Venture* magazine for its Index of Venture Capital Activity. The index is compiled by a monthly telephone survey of 25 leading US venture capital firms. The definitions of Stages I, II and III are the same as used previously, i.e.:

Stage	Description	Sales	Profits
I	Seed/start-up	No	No
II	Second Stage	Yes	No
III	Development	Yes	Yes

The MIC Licensing Board encouraged the MICs to seek out and invest in Stage I and II investments. The MIC Act did not allow MICs to invest in leveraged buy-outs. The mix for the MICs as of 30 June 1989 is shown in Table 23.3.

Step 3—evaluation of investment

The Tyebjee & Bruno paper, using the latest statistical techniques, exhaustively analysed the decision variables used in an evaluation. The authors found that five factors from an original list of 23 variables often mentioned by non-players were unused or dismissed. They were:

- patentability of the product, this was probably a result of the general and complete disillusionment by most of industry with the patent process;
- raw material availability;
- production capability;
- tax benefits, because the venture capitalist would be looking at the investment to provide capital gain and not a tax shelter; and
- reduction of portfolio risk, instead of; investments were considered on a one at a time basis.

By contrast, the Tyebjee & Bruno study found five factors that were mentioned time and again by the US venture capitalists. They were:

- market attractiveness (++);
- product differentiation (+);

Table 23.1 Effect of head office location on investments

Name	Location of head office	% of investee businesses	% of funds invested
Austech	NSW	71.5	71.9
APT	VIC	52.2	33.0
BTIL	NSW	77.7	71.4
CVC	NSW	83.2	66.4
CP Ventures	VIC	40.0	37.3
First MIC	NSW	61.9	60.2
Samic	SA	52.9	58.3
Stinoc	WA	47.0	32.4
Techniche	QLD	28.6	44.0
Western Pacific	VIC	40.0	28.8
Westintech	WA	100.0	100.0

Source: MIC Annual Report 1988–89

- cash-out potential;
- environmental threat resistance (obsolescence, low barriers to entry)(–); and
- managerial capabilities(– –).

The signs in the brackets refer to relative strength.

Investors are looking at both return and risk. The first three factors raise the potential rate of return while the second two increase the likelihood of failure.

By contrast and probably reflecting a combination of inexperience, small market size and limited market information, Australian venture capital participants tend to focus less on market factors. The Ernst & Whinney survey uncovered in order of importance:

management capability   30%
product   22%

Table 23.2 US investment activity

Business stage	Funds invested		Number of deals	Average	
	$M	%		%	$M
I	144	19	227	17	0.64
II	112	15	94	7	1.19
III	315	41	984	72	0.32
LBO	193	25	55	4	3.51
Total	764	100	1360	100	

profit history	16%
balance sheet	13%
security	9%
other	11%

Step 4—structuring the deal

If the evaluation proves satisfactory, the next stage is structuring the deal. No methodology for valuation is generally acceptable but the earlier chapters on structuring and valuation describe some of the more common techniques. A secret of venture capital is to use the structure of the financing to focus entrepreneurs on reaching the goals set out in the business plan. The approach differs whether the investment is a start-up or second stage.

For the start-up the secret is to tranche the investment. If an entrepreneur requires about $750 000, then instead of investing the amount in one tranche the funding should be divided into, say, three tranches of about $250 000 each. The investment of the first tranche occurs immediately and the second and third tranches only follow on the achievement of some mutually agreed project milestones.

For the second-stage investment, venture capitalists may adopt a structure known as 'reverse tranching'. Assume an investment requires $1.2 million for 46 per cent of the company post investment and the company is expected to be profitable within two years. The company intends to list in four years. One possible structure is to invest, say, 25 per cent in ordinary shares and 21 per cent in redeemable preference shares. At the end of the second, third and fourth years, 7 per cent of the redeemable preference shares can be redeemed and replaced with bonus shares for the entrepreneurs if mutually agreed profit targets are reached.

Table 23.3 MIC investment activity 30 June 1989

Business stage	Funds invested		Number of deals	Average	
	$ M	%		%	$ M
I	128.6	74	111	75	1.158
II	31.3	18	26	18	1.203
III	15.0	8	11	7	1.136
Total	174.9	100	148	100	

The reverse tranche structure is a good structure for introducing reality into the projections of the entrepreneurs. Typically the initial conservative profit projection estimates are:

Years	1	2	3	4
Profit ($million)	0	3	6	9

When the concept of the reverse tranche is introduced and accepted, the profit projections are usually revised:

Years	1	2	3	4
Profit ($million)	0	0.1	0.2	0.3

The art of structuring then becomes one of agreeing on profit growth that is sensible and achievable.

By using tranches the venture capitalist can achieve the best platform for a successful listing—quality of earnings. Tranching also has the important benefit of focusing the mind of the entrepreneur on the key objective of business, namely growth in profits.

Step 5—post-investment activities

The essence of venture capital is that it should not just be money but should add value in other ways, which have been detailed in Chapter 20. For the fund manager whose time is limited the key activities may be summarised as follows:

- *Recruitment of founders and management:* Since entrepreneurs often start from an engineering or production background and lack either marketing or financial skills, venture capitalists can play an important role in staff recruitment.
- *Sourcing additional funds:* Venture capitalists play a key role in sourcing additional funds, such as equity, debt or lines of credit. They should aim at leveraging their equity investment by an equivalent amount of debt and government grants.
- *Acting as a devil's advocate:* Since small-business people walk alone and have no sounding boards, venture capitalists act as devil's advocates. By simply reading many business plans one begins to develop a good 'feel' for the keys to

success—what the financial ratios should be, whether the market projections are realistic, and so on.

- *Fostering the correct climate:* This may be defined as the combination of marketing enthusiasm and attention to costs that is not found in large companies. It is important to prevent the Maserati complex developing—this is when the first purchase of a newly funded company is a Maserati for the entrepreneur.
- *Providing credibility for big sales:* Since small start-up companies lack status, having a venture capitalist as a referee, especially if the company the venture capitalist represents has a high profile, can be most helpful.
- *Advising on legal protection:* Since intellectual property rights are unfamiliar to many lawyers, and licensing agreements, patents and trademarks are expensive to arrange, venture capitalists can be useful and helpful advisers and prevent costly mistakes.
- *Exit mechanisms:* Since the procedures of underwriting, choosing a broker, prospectus preparation and other exit mechanisms may be unfamiliar to entrepreneurs, venture capitalists also provide negotiating support in these areas.

Conclusion

In his excellent book *Venture Capital,* upon which many of the concepts in this book are based, A.D. Silver identifies eight functions in venture capital investing:

- deal generation
- due diligence
- structuring the terms and conditions
- syndication
- monitoring
- adding value
- selling out and exiting
- portfolio management.

We have covered the first seven activities in some detail and will discuss portfolio management in the last chapter.

What qualifications and skills does one need to be a venture capitalist? One essential is a combination of corporate finance, underwriting and syndication skills derived from either stockbroking or merchant banking. Another requirement would be market analysis, investment appraisal and due diligence skills. Someone who has worked in either security analysis, portfolio management, corporate lending, market research, corporate planning or product development would have these skills. The final skills of monitoring and added value would come from working as a general manager in a company or division of a multinational.

Another issue is how many managers there should be in a venture capital fund. The venture capitalist with the best track record in the US, Arthur Rock, found two was too many and works on his own. Silver considers three the optimum number because a larger number slows response and agreement time on an opportunity. He also considers the optimal fund size is between $20 million and $40 million. He regards an amount above $40 million as too large and likely to cause the manager to make injudicious investments under pressure to lay off funds.

The figures from the 1986–87 MIC report show the MICs employed 58 managers for eleven funds managing 111 investments. The typical ratio for hands-on management is about one half-day per week which accounts for the limit of five to eight investments per manager. The MICs on this evidence would appear to have been overstaffed.

Finally, what should be the degree of personal financial involvement by the venture capital managers themselves? The classic question asked of the portfolio manager is, 'Would you put your own money in this company?' For the venture capitalist the question should be restated, 'How much of your own money are you going to put in this deal?' Just as entrepreneurs should have hurt money at stake so should the managers of a venture capital fund. Obviously the amount must be sensible as the recommending manager will have investments in about half a dozen deals. The willingness of venture capital fund managers to invest their own capital is perhaps the strongest recommendation they can make for an investment proposal.

24 Portfolio management

In this final chapter we shall discuss the portfolio management aspects of a venture capital fund. Among venture capital funds there is a spectrum of management involvement ranging from active hands-on to almost pseudo-institutional hands-off investing. Hands-off management is an alternative for the larger fund but most venture capital funds in Australia are small and adopt a hands-on style. Hands-on management is the traditional style and it is the one discussed in this book.

We shall compare a traditional portfolio, investing in either bonds or equities, with a hands-on venture capital fund. The first difference in managing the two types of portfolio is the marketability of investments. It makes no difference if equity or bond managers make poor or brilliant decisions; either way they can recover some, or a significant multiple, of their capital. On the other hand the venture capital investor has difficulty with liquidity—the public listing market and the company sale market are both slow in operation. Listings can take up to six months, company acquisitions from three to twelve months.

The compensation venture capitalists must have for this lack of liquidity is control. If the venture starts to veer away from the business plan, venture capitalists should have built into the shareholders' agreement enough controls and devices to ensure they can take remedial action. The chapters on structuring and post-investment activities describe the techniques. Failure to include control mechanisms enshrined in formal and legally binding agreements will soon lead to portfolio loss and disaster.

The problem for venture capitalists managing a portfolio is that if many investments go wrong concurrently they will soon run out of time to handle the fires. What venture capitalists must do is diversify this risk by spreading their investments among different industries and among companies at different stages of development, and spreading them over time.

Diversification among different industry sectors is difficult in Australia. The primary industry sector, mining and agriculture, is high-risk. You either strike oil or you don't. Agriculture is similarly high-risk—with new ventures such as aquaculture suffering high development risk and poor track records. Commodity prices are volatile and the fluctuations can destroy the quality of earnings so crucial to raising further rounds of funds.

The manufacturing sector in Australia, especially in electronics, is by international standards small and weak. The active government assistance in this area is negated by the excessive add-on costs and the poor taxation structure, which raises excessive revenue from income tax and so penalises overtime.

The services sector, while fast growing, still tends to be small and fragmented. The small size of the domestic market and the 'tyranny of distance' limits the potential of Australian service companies.

The MIC Licensing Board annual reports provide the most detailed analysis of venture capital activity in Australia. Table 24.1 shows how the $175 million so far invested by the MICs is distributed according to industry.

A US venture capital company would probably show a similar distribution except that it would probably have invested about 20–25 per cent of its portfolio in leveraged buy-outs and 10–20 per cent in consumer businesses, especially ones based on franchising.

The next form of diversification is by stage of development. Table 24.2 shows how the average US venture capital fund diversifies risk by stage of company. For deals done, the average investment is smaller the earlier the stage of investment. However the later stage deals are usually syndicated, so while the size of investment increases the individual investment per fund decreases. The portfolio breakdown is shown in Table 24.3. The

Table 24.1 MIC investment by industry

Computer hardware & components	17.2%
Computer software	7.4%
Medical equipment & products	16.3%
Communications systems & services	9.0%
Other electronic products	13.3%
Biotechnology	5.3%
Other manufacturing	18.9%
Other services	12.6%

Table 24.2   US investment by stage of company

Stage I (no sales no profits)	20%
Stage II (sales no profits)	15%
Stage III (sales and profits)	40%
Leveraged buy-outs	25%

Table 24.3   US deals done by stage of company

Stage I (no sales no profits)	27%
Stage II (sales no profits)	8%
Stage III (sales and profits)	70%
Leveraged buy-outs	5%

Table 24.4   MIC investment by stage of company

	% of funds invested	% of number of investments
Stage I	69	72
Stage II	19	18
Stage III	12	10

MIC Licensing Board 1988–89 Annual Report aggregated the investments of the eleven MICs by stage of development, as shown in Table 24.4.

No LBO investments occurred because of prohibition by the MIC Act. MICs have been actively encouraged to invest in early stage companies. Early stage investments take more of a venture capitalist's time and this is probably the main reason for the overstaffing mentioned in the previous chapter. Early stage investments are also riskier. The management task facing the MIC with large monitoring costs and a risky portfolio is difficult. It is probably a significant reason for the low stock market rating accorded to most MIC companies. Another means of diversification is by geography. While for the equity and bond manager investing in overseas markets has become increasingly popular, geographical diversification for venture capitalists is less so. As mentioned earlier, a golden rule of venture capital is to invest within one hour's travel of the investment. This principle usually outweighs the need for geographical diversification. Venture capitalists usually achieve some diversification by being passive syndicate partners in interstate investments. Unfortunately, as mentioned before, Australia has only two cities of sufficient market size to support a start-up. Moreover, according to the MIC Licensing Board reports, New South Wales has twice the activity of Victoria. Hence a fund based outside Victoria or New South Wales suffers from both inadequate deal flow and the need to invest much of the portfolio away from the management offices.

The final and perhaps most important form of diversification is the time of investment. Venture capitalists should try to spread out their portfolio and not concentrate their investments into too short a timespan. Fashions change. In Australia in the early 1980s energy resources were popular and agriculture was a leper. However by the late 1980s the wool price was at an all-time high while coal mines, developed in the intervening years, were dragging down the earnings of many companies.

While venture capitalists will find it difficult to buy straw hats in winter, they should not focus too much on the hot industry of the moment nor listen too closely to the forecasters of the time. When venture capital started in Australia in 1983, IBM was flavour of the month because of the success of the personal computer. Industry experts thought poorly of DEC because of the disaster with the Rainbow. The theme of all the computer forecasting seminars at the time was how could IBM possibly be stopped? The forecasters were in reality tolling the bell. The PC would become a price-cutting market with few companies except those US corporations with wide-use software making serious money. On the other hand DEC increased market share with its powerful mid-range computers, inter-range compatibility and networking skills.

Cash management trust managers who invest primarily in 90-day bank bills can effectively index their fund by splitting it into thirteen equal amounts. A thirteenth of the fund is invested every week in new issues and the bills held till maturity. Venture capitalists should adopt the same philosophy and aim at developing a pipeline of deals with an average time in the pipeline of about four years. The corollary of this principle is that if the maximum spread of investments a venture capitalist should be handling is eight, then he or she should be completing about two new deals a year. On completion value should be added and the investment driven to a public listing within three years. Natural slippage will mean the average time to exit will slide to about four years till takeout. This concept of buying into companies, increasing their value and then exiting is not new.

Figure 24.1 MIC funds allocation 1984–91

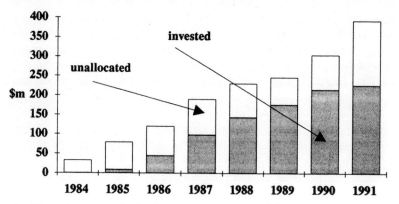

As Silver has noted, the best proponents of this investment cycle were the British merchant banks in the late nineteenth century; they developed it into an art form.

Another portfolio decision to be made is how much of the fund should be kept liquid. Pension fund managers usually adopt a strategy of investing 10 per cent of funds under management in money market instruments. Venture capitalists with the rest of their portfolio locked up in illiquid investments need to keep a higher proportion in liquid investments; experience suggests about one quarter is correct. Figure 24.1 shows the aggregate uninvested funds of the MICs during the life of the program. The MICs appear to have kept one-third of the funds in reserve. This figure should be taken with caution, however, because some of the funds raised were in the form of convertible redeemable preference shares, which meant the fund could safely invest only the interest generated by the equity subscription but not the capital.

The liquidity is needed for follow-on funding. One rule of venture capital investing is that high-growth companies need at least twice the amount of funding initially estimated in the business plan. The difficulty for venture capitalists lies in establishing whether the need is because of failure or success. The acid test is whether with the follow-on funding the venture capitalists can attract new syndicate partners. If not, they must carefully consider whether to make the follow-on investment. Experience recommends not, because it would probably be throwing good money after bad. What may happen is that the investment goes on a drip feed, whereby it is given monthly cash amounts while the management and the incumbent venture capitalists look for additional funding. Even on the drip feed the venture capitalists should set careful limits.

Another problem with venture capital funds is that the lemons fall before the plums. Assume a venture capitalist has made two equal investments and that after a year both require funds—one because it has sold nothing and the other because it is growing faster than expected and needs additional working capital. New investors are queuing up to invest in the latter company at a 75 per cent increase above the initial post-funding valuation. None wishes to invest in the former company. The incumbent investor must concede defeat and write off the first investment as a lemon. However, his total portfolio will now suffer a loss in value. If the second investment shows the same increase of 75 per cent at the end of the third year the compounding effect will more than compensate for the lemon. Nevertheless, the plum still falls after the lemon. This rule is one reason venture capital funds in the US do not list on the share markets—because of the drop in net tangible assets for the first two to three years.

Another problem with some venture capital firms is the search for the big winner. One of the first venture capital firms was American Research & Development, mentioned earlier. Founded in 1947, ARD was very successful with its initial investment in Digital Equipment Corporation, which over a sixteen-year period had compound growth of 84 per cent. The original $70 000 investment was subsequently worth $350 million. The success of DEC dominated the performance of the ARD portfolio. In time the prevalent venture capital strategy became the search for the king hit.

It is possible to simulate a model of a venture capital portfolio using a spreadsheet, as shown in Table 24.5. In this model it is assumed that the portfolio begins on day one with ten equal investments and runs for five years. The objective of the portfolio is to show a 25 per cent compound growth over the period. It is assumed that certain investments are going to fall over and that only 10 per cent of the original asset will be salvaged (the lemons). Figure 24.2 shows the rate of return needed from the remaining investments (the plums) in order to achieve the overall portfolio objective.

Table 24.2 shows that if nine of the ten investments are lemons the remaining investment must achieve a compound annual return of 97 per cent. The relationship is not linear. If only six lemons occur, the average return required from the remaining plums is 55 per cent. This suggests that venture capitalists might better spend their time on three or four investments than on trying to find one king hit. A corollary of adopting such a strategy is a limitation on the number of investments a venture capitalist can manage.

Reducing the portfolio rate of return objective has a negligible effect on the slope of the curve or required rates of return. As recorded above, a portfolio with an objective of 25 per cent needs a 97 per cent return from one remaining asset and 72 per cent if two remain, making a difference of 25 per cent. If the rate of return is increased to 35 per cent, the required rates of return are 113 per cent and 86 per cent respectively, resulting in a difference of 27 per cent.

Another rule of venture capital management is that the more patient the venture capitalist, the better the return on his or her portfolio. This rule sits uncomfortably with most institutional portfolio managers, who are influenced by quarterly surveys and advisers' reports. Yet the model supports this approach. If the same overall return objective is kept but the time horizon of the portfolio is lengthened, then the required rate of return curve lessens substantially. As an example, the required rate of return for a single remaining asset in a five-year 25 per cent target return portfolio is 97 per cent. If the portfolio termination

Table 24.5   Venture capital portfolio model

Initial value	Required return	Period (years)	Final value	Salvage ratio
10	25%	5	30.52	10%

Lemons	Remaining final value	Remaining initial value	Required return (%)	Difference (%)
1	30.4	9.0	27.6	
2	30.3	8.0	30.5	3.0
3	30.2	7.0	34.0	3.4
4	30.1	6.0	38.1	4.1
5	30.0	5.0	43.1	5.0
6	29.9	4.0	49.6	6.4
7	29.8	3.0	58.3	8.8
8	29.7	2.0	71.6	13.3
9	29.6	1.0	96.9	25.4

Figure 24.2 Venture capital model—required rate of return

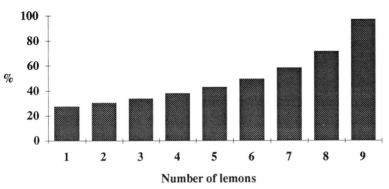

date extends to seven years, the required rate of return falls to 73 per cent.

As indicated above, venture capitalists should make sure they gain control over the investment if it fails to perform. Many venture capital textbooks expound this rule as a key clause to be contained in the shareholders' agreement. As venture capitalists often have the minority position, the disaster clause usually contains some trigger point such as an asset/liability ratio being breached. Venture capitalists either gain control of the board, are assigned the voting rights of the entrepreneurs, or appoint a governing director. They spend much time negotiating this clause with entrepreneurs.

After being assured by the venture capitalists that he or she only wants a minority position, the entrepreneur then finds disaster clauses inserted demanding total control. It is debatable whether the conflict is necessary. If the model is run with the salvage ratio set at 90 per cent rather than 10 per cent, it makes little difference to the gradient of the required rate of return curve; it just goes to slightly lower values. If only one asset remains the required rate of return drops from 97 per cent to 86 per cent. Thus venture capitalists, instead of concentrating their efforts on the disaster clause or subsequently trying to resuscitate the lemons, might be better advised to cut their losses. The venture capital philosophy of Kleiner-Perkins, regarded by many as the number one venture capital firm in the US, supports this belief.

Eugene Kleiner, one of the founders of Silicon Valley, has been quoted as saying: 'There is a time when panic is the appropriate response. However, if you make a mistake, get out quickly, just get it over because otherwise it takes so much time.' On the other hand, replacing the chief executive officer may be the one change that a company needs to survive and grow.

Appendix A Pro-forma cash flow projection, income statements and balance sheets

Operating cash flows	: Mon 1	12 :	Year 1 :	Year 2 :	Year 3 :
Cash receipts	:	:	:	:	:
Sales	:	:	:	:	:
Govt grants – EMDG	:	:	:	:	:
– GIRD	:	:	:	:	:
– BOUNTY	:	:	:	:	:
Royalties/Other	:	:	:	:	:
Total cash receipts	:	:	:	:	:
Variable payments	:	:	:	:	:
Staff costs:	:	:	:	:	:
Salaries & wages	:	:	:	:	:
Payroll tax	:	:	:	:	:
Superannuation	:	:	:	:	:
Other	:	:	:	:	:
Freight & cartage	:	:	:	:	:
Stock	:	:	:	:	:
Sales tax	:	:	:	:	:
Total variable payments	:	:	:	:	:
Gross margin	:	:	:	:	:
Fixed payments	:	:	:	:	:

Staff costs:					
Salaries & wages	..	..	..	..	..
Payroll tax	..	..	..	..	..
Superannuation	..	..	..	..	..
Other	..	..	..	..	..
Service costs:					
Commissions	..	..	..	..	..
Motor vehicles	..	..	..	..	..
Travel & entertain.	..	..	..	..	..
Promotion and advert.	..	..	..	..	..
Other	..	..	..	..	..
Facilities:					
Rent	..	..	..	..	..
Rates & land tax	..	..	..	..	..
Leasing	..	..	..	..	..
Computer	..	..	..	..	..
Repairs and maintenance	..	..	..	..	..
Other	..	..	..	..	..
Other costs					
Admin. (Acct,bank fees)	..	..	..	..	..
Insurance	..	..	..	..	..
Electricity	..	..	..	..	..
Telephone & telex	..	..	..	..	..
Printing, post & stat.	..	..	..	..	..
Interest	..	..	..	..	..
Other	..	..	..	..	..
Total fixed payments	..	..	..	..	..

	:Mon 1		12 :	Year 1 :	Year 2 :	Year 3 :
Non P & L payments	:		:	:	:	:
Capital expend.	:		:	:	:	:
Tax/FBT/other	:		:	:	:	:
Total cash payments	:		:	:	:	:
Surplus/(deficit)	:		:	:	:	:
Cumulative operating C/F	:		:	:	:	:

Financing cash flows	:Mon 1		12 :	Year 1 :	Year 2 :	Year 3 :
Debt	:		:	:	:	:
Equity	:		:	:	:	:
Less:	:		:	:	:	:
Debt principal repay.	:		:	:	:	:
Dividends	:		:	:	:	:
Total financing C/F	:		:	:	:	:
Net cash flow	:		:	:	:	:
Opening balance–cash	:		:	:	:	:
Closing balance–cash	:		:	:	:	:
Overdraft limit $	:		:	:	:	:

Non-cash expenses	: Mon 1	12 :	Year 1 :	Year 2 :	Year 3 :
Depreciation	:	:	:	:	:
Leave provisions	:	:	:	:	:
Bad debt provisons	:	:	:	:	:
Stock provisions	:	:	:	:	:
Tax provisions	:	:	:	:	:
Total non-cash expenses	:	:	:	:	:

Projected P & Ls	: Year 1 ….		Balance sheets	Year 1 ….
Sales	:		Current assets:	
Other operating income	:		Cash	
	:		Deposits	
Total revenue	:		Stock	
	:		Other	
less: COGS	:			
Opening stock	:		Total current assets	
+Purchase	:			
−Closing stock	:		Fixed assets	
Cost of goods sold	:			
			Investments	
Gross profit	:		Intangibles	
Total expenses	:		Total assets	

Operating profit (loss) : _____

+/- Non-operating items : _____

Profit before tax : _____

Tax : _____

Profit after tax : _____

Current liabilities:
Bank overdraft
Creditors
Provisions   −Tax
             −Dividends
Loans
Other

Non-current liabs:
Loans
Leave provisions
Other
Total liabilities
Paid-up capital
Retain, earn.−Open. bal
Net profit
less dividends
Other
Shareholders' funds

Appendix B Sample spreadsheet for investment monitoring

Actuals :	JUL	AUG	SEP	OCT	NOV	DEC	JAN	FEB	MAR	APR	MAY	JUN :	YTD
Revenues :	1200	1400	1500	1300	1100	1000	800	1200	1500	1800	1400	1900 :	16100
Gross margin :	650	800	850	800	600	600	450	700	900	1000	800	950 :	9100
Oper income :	-100	80	150	0	-70	0	-300	100	200	300	500	800 :	1660
Net profit/(loss) :	-60	48	90	0	-42	0	-180	60	120	180	300	480 :	996

Budget :	JUL	AUG	SEP	OCT	NOV	DEC	JAN	FEB	MAR	APR	MAY	JUN :	BUD
Revenues :	1000	1100	1200	1300	1400	1000	700	1400	1500	1600	1700	1800 :	15700
Gross margin :	500	550	600	650	700	500	350	700	750	800	850	900 :	7850
Oper income :	-50	-10	30	70	110	-100	-260	80	120	160	200	240 :	590
Net profit/(loss) :	-30	-6	18	42	66	-60	-156	48	72	96	120	144 :	354

Actuals :	JUL	AUG	SEP	OCT	NOV	DEC	JAN	FEB	MAR	APR	MAY	JUN :	BUD
Cash on hand :	10	20	5	160	10	10	5	5	100	5	5	900 :	0
Debtors :	2600	2400	2800	2500	2700	2800	2800	2400	2800	4000	3500	3600 :	5000
Stock :	3900	3800	3600	3600	3600	3600	3800	3800	3800	3600	4300	3900 :	4300
Current assets :	6510	6220	6405	6260	6310	6410	6605	6205	6700	7605	7805	8400 :	9300
Total assets :	7510	7220	7405	7260	7310	7410	7605	7205	7700	8605	8805	9400 :	10500
Short term debt :	400	0	200	0	50	100	400	100	0	900	150	0 :	700
Creditors :	1100	1100	1000	900	700	800	700	600	700	700	900	1200 :	1800
Provisions :	400	420	440	460	480	500	520	540	560	580	600	620 :	750
Current liabilities :	1900	1520	1640	1360	1230	1400	1620	1240	1260	2180	1650	1820 :	3250

	JUL	AUG	SEP	OCT	NOV	DEC	JAN	FEB	MAR	APR	MAY	JUN	BUD
Long term debt	0	0	0	0	0	0	0	0	0	0	0	0	0
Total liabilities	1900	1520	1640	1360	1230	1400	1620	1240	1260	2180	1650	1820	3250
Total equity	5610	5700	5765	5900	6080	6010	5985	5965	6440	6425	7155	7580	7250
Working capital	4610	4700	4765	4900	5080	5010	4985	4965	5440	5425	6155	6580	
Int gen funds	0	24	48	72	96	-30	-126	78	102	126	455	388	
Delta W/C	0	90	65	135	180	-70	-25	-20	475	-15	730	425	
Fixed assets inv	10	10	10	10	10	10	10	10	10	10	10	10	
Opr. cash flow	-10	-76	-27	-73	-94	30	-111	88	-383	131	-285	-47	

Ratio analysis	JUL	AUG	SEP	OCT	NOV	DEC	JAN	FEB	MAR	APR	MAY	JUN	BUD
Fixed costs	750	720	700	800	670	600	750	600	700	700	300	150	7260
% gross margin	54%	57%	57%	62%	55%	60%	56%	58%	60%	56%	57%	50%	50%
Break even	1385	1260	1235	1300	1228	1000	1333	1029	1167	1260	525	300	14520
Margin of safety	87%	111%	121%	100%	90%	100%	60%	117%	129%	143%	267%	633%	108%
Stock in sales-months	3.25	2.71	2.40	2.77	3.27	3.60	4.75	3.17	2.53	2.00	3.07	2.05	3.29
Debtors in sales-months	2.17	1.71	1.87	1.92	2.45	2.80	3.50	2.00	1.87	2.22	2.50	1.89	3.82
Creds. in sales-months	0.92	0.79	0.67	0.69	0.64	0.80	0.88	0.50	0.47	0.39	0.64	0.63	1.38
Number of staff	147	142	139	138	142	143	144	145	147	153	159	160	156
Ann. sales/emp.	98	118	129	113	93	84	67	99	122	141	106	143	103
% net income	-8%	6%	10%	0%	-6%	0%	-38%	8%	13%	17%	36%	42%	4%
% return on equity	-21%	17%	31%	0%	-14%	0%	-60%	20%	37%	56%	84%	127%	98%
Asset turn	1.92	2.33	2.43	2.15	1.81	1.62	1.26	2.00	2.34	2.51	1.91	2.43	1.50
Gearing	7%	0%	3%	0%	1%	2%	7%	2%	0%	14%	2%	0%	10%
Current ratio	3.43	4.09	3.91	4.60	5.13	4.58	4.08	5.00	5.32	3.49	4.73	4.62	2.86
Acid test	1.37	1.59	1.71	1.96	2.20	2.01	1.73	1.94	2.30	1.84	2.12	2.47	1.54

Bibliography

Brandt, S. C., *Entrepreneuring, The Ten Commandments for Building a Growth Company*, New American Library, New York, 1982.

Brophy, D. J., 'Flow of Venture Capital 1977–1980', in *Frontiers of Entrepreneurship research* K.H. Vesper (ed.), Babson College, Mass. 1981, pp. 246–80.

Bureau of Industry Economics, 'The public interest IR & D program', Program Evaluation Report 1, Australian Government Printing Service, Canberra, 1985.

—— 'Evaluation of public support for industrial research and development', Conference Papers and Proceedings Canberra 2 May 1986, Australian Government Printing Service, Canberra, 1986.

—— 'Review of venture capital in Australia and the MIC Program', Program Evaluation Report 4, Australian Government Printing Service, Canberra, 1987.

Churchill, N. C. and Lewis V.L., 'The five stages of small business growth', *Harvard Business Review*, May–June 1983

Department of Industry, Technology and Commerce, *Bringing the market to bear on research*, Australian Government Publishing Service, November 1991.

Diamond, S. C., *Leveraged Buyouts*, Dow Jones-Irwin, Homewood, Illinois, 1985.

Drucker, P. F., *Innovation and Entrepreneurship*, William Heinemann, London, 1985.

Ernst & Whinney, 'Annual Australian Venture Capital Survey', Sydney, 1988.

Fast, Dr N.D., 'New Technology Ventures for Corporate Growth', paper presented at a forum held in Canberra, 1983.

Ford, J., *Scitech Technology Directory 1987–88 Edition*, Scitech Publications Pty Ltd, Canberra, 1987.

Fox, A., *Australia's New Entrepreneurs*, Enterprise Australia Publications, Sydney, 1986.

Hartley, R. F., *Bullseyes and Blunders, Stories of Business Success & Failure*, John Wiley & Sons, New York, 1987.

Industry Research and Development Board, *Innovation in Australia*, Australian Government Publishing Service, July 1991.

Kotkin, J., 'Why smart companies are saying no to venture capital', INC August 1984.

Lipper III, A., *Investing in Private Companies*, Dow Jones-Irwin, Homewood, Illinois, 1984.

Lorenz, T., *Venture Capital Today*, Woodhead-Faulkner, Cambridge, 1985.

Malone, M. S., *The Big Score, The Billion Dollar Story of Silicon Valley*, Doubleday & Co, Garden City, New York, 1985.

Management and Investment Companies Licensing Board, *Annual Reports 1984–91*, Australian Government Publishing Service, Canberra.

Mille, R. and Côté, M, 'Growing the next Silicon Valley', *Harvard Business Review*, July–August 1985.

O'Neill, G.K., *The Technology Edge*, Simon and Schuster, New York, 1983.

Rogers, E.M. and Larsen, J.K., *Silicon Valley Fever*, Basic Books, Inc., New York, 1984.

Ryan, A., *Technology Assistance Directory*, 1988 Prestige Edition, The Licensing Executives Society (LES ANZ INC), Sydney.

Silver, A.D., *The Entrepreneurial Life*, John Wiley & Sons, New York 1986.

——*Venture Capital—The Complete Guide for Investors*, John Wiley & Sons, New York, 1983.

Taylor, A.L., 'Making a Mint overnight', *Time*, 23 January 1984.

Tyebjee, T.T. and Bruno, A.V., 'A model of venture capitalist investment activity', *Management Science*, 1984, Vol 30, No. 9, pp. 1051–66.

Timmons, Dr J. A., 'Venture Capital: More than Money', *Pratts Guide to Venture Capital Sources*, 8th ed. Venture Economics, Inc., Massachusetts.

Wang, Dr A., *Lessons, An Autobiography*, Addison-Wesley Publishing, Reading, Massachusetts, 1986.

Wilson, J.W., *The New Venturers, Inside the High-Stakes World of Venture Capital*, Addison-Wesley Publishing, Reading, Massachusetts, 1985.

Index